MW01290652

CALIFORNIA
NOTARY PUBLIC EXAM

Angelo Tropea

"Notaries Public...hold an office which can trace its origins back to ancient Rome when they were called *scribae*, *tabellius or notarius*. They are easily the oldest continuing branch of the legal profession worldwide."

ISBN 13: 978-1539554646
ISBN 10: 1539554643

Please note that the questions and answers in this book review
the subject matter of the relevant California statutes, codes,
rules, the Notary Public Handbook 2022, published by the
California Secretary of State, and other sources. They are
meant to be used as study aids and not legal reference.
The primary sources of official legal reference are the laws and
codes themselves.

The official "Notary Public Handbook" (Published by Dr. Shirley
N. Weber, Secretary of State, Notary Public Section 2022)" is
available for free online at:

https://notary.cdn.sos.ca.gov/forms/notary-handbook-current.pdf

----

Please note that although the author has made every effort to
ensure that the information in this book was correct at press
time, the author and publisher do not assume and hereby
disclaim any liability to any party for any loss, damage, or
disruption caused by errors or omissions, whether such errors or
omissions result from negligence, accident, or any other cause.
Also, please note that this book is intended as a study aid and
not as a substitute for the official courses and materials that are
available. All references to California codes and statutes are
edited and unofficial and are not to be used as legal reference.
The official codes, statutes, and notary public handbook are all
available for free on the web. Also, please check for any
amendments to the laws and fees.

CONTENTS

THE AIM OF THIS BOOK

This book is designed to serve as an effective study tool and to serve as a companion (and not a replacement) of the study materials of the official courses.

Please note that the primary sources of legal reference are the laws themselves and the official "Notary Public Handbook" (Published by Dr. Shirley N. Weber, Secretary of State, Notary Public Section 2022)" which is available for free online at:

https://notary.cdn.sos.ca.gov/forms/notary-handbook-current.pdf

The publication is excellent. It contains the information you need to know.

The aim of this book is to complement the official publications by highlighting important points and offering study tools to help you better prepare for the exam and make it easier for you to become a more knowledgeable and professional practicing notary public.

_____

This book provides

1. True/False and fill-in "Quick Questions" to help you remember important facts and definitions.

2. Multiple choice questions to help you practice for the notary public exam.

3. Practice exams to help you to further solidify your knowledge of the laws and rules relevant to notaries.

We believe that the combination of the above will provide the tools and the required practice to help you achieve your goal of passing with a high grade the notary public

Made in the USA
San Bernardino, CA
10 March 2017

exam and also increase your understanding and appreciation of laws important to notaries public.

A Notary Public Application form and information regarding the appointment process can be found on the California Secretary of State's website at:

http://www.sos.ca.gov/notary/

HOW TO USE THIS BOOK

There are probably as many ways to study successfully as there are people. However, in the more than thirty years of preparing study materials and conducting classes for civil service exams, I have found that certain methods seem to work better than others with the great majority of students. The following are time tested suggestions that you might want to consider as you incorporate this book in the study plan that is best for you.

SUGGESTIONS

In addition to attending a required class:

1. First read the notaries public handbook.

2. If you wish, you can read the actual sections of law that are referenced in the handbook. They are also available for free on the internet, including the California Government Code. (Just search for "California Government Code.")

3. Also, make sure you are confident with all the relevant legal terms. They will form the basis of your understanding of the law and help you later when you are a practicing notary public.

4. Try the "Quick Questions." They are designed to emphasize important facts. Do not go on to the multiple-

choice questions until you have mastered these questions. Read the additional information after some answers to reinforce important facts.

5. Now tackle the multiple-choice questions. On the actual test you may have around 45 multiple choice questions.

6. When you think you are ready, take the Practice Exams.

Study every day. Take this book with you – and make it your friend!

––––––––––––

ABBREVIATIONS USED IN THIS BOOK

To help make this book less wordy, we use the following abbreviations and notations:

notary = "notary public"

CGC = "California Government Code"

Secretary of State = "California Secretary of State"

his = "his or her" or "his/her"

ID = Identification document

Notary Handbook = California Notary Handbook

The word "section" as used in ("CGC section 1129") is omitted).

LEGAL TERMS

The following are useful legal terms. They contain editorial comments intended to jump-start your understanding of the words. For official definitions, please consult a legal dictionary.

Acknowledgment – is a declaration that is made before an official (example: notary public) that under the person's free act and deed he did execute the instrument.

"He paid the notary for taking the acknowledgment."

Administrator – An administrator of an estate is appointed by the court and empowers him to manage the affairs of the decedent (dead person). The court appoints an administrator where a person dies without leaving a will or leaves a will without naming an executor.

"The Judge stated that because the deceased did not name anyone in the will to act as executor, the court had to appoint an administrator to handle the affairs of the decedent."

Affiant – An affidavit (a sworn to or affirmed written statement) is signed by a person called the affiant.

"Because of religious reasons, the affiant affirmed instead of swearing an oath before he signed the statement."

Affidavit – is a signed statement that is sworn to by the person signing it. An affidavit is sworn to in front of a notary public or other officer with authority to administer an oath.

"The person signed the affidavit in front of the notary."

Affirmation – A person who does not want to take an oath (because of religious, ethical, or other reasons) may affirm as to the truthfulness of his statements. The act of affirming is called the affirmation. An affirmation is just as binding as an oath.

"The person made the affirmation instead of swearing an oath because of religious reasons."

Apostile – An apostile is an authentication of a notarized document to be used internationally.

"She obtained an apostile of the document so she could use it in the Mexican courts."

Attest – To attest is to be present at the execution of a written instrument and also to subscribe (sign) the written instrument as a witness to the execution of the instrument.

"The witness will be present and will attest to the execution of the written instrument."

Attestation clause – As it refers to wills, an attestation clause is the written portion at the end of a will where the witnesses attest that the will was executed in front of them, and also state the procedural manner of the execution of the will.

"The attestation clause must be located at the end of the will."

Bill of sale – A bill of sale is a written document that is given by the vendor (seller of personal property) to the vendee (buyer). It passes title from the vendor to the vendee.

"After Charles signed the bill of sale, the buyer officially took ownership of the car."

Chattel – Chattel means property that is personal in nature, such as household goods. Chattel does NOT include real property (land, buildings).

"In addition to the land and building, the seller included a list of chattel located on the property that would also be included in the sale of the property."

Chattel paper – A written obligation to pay money for specific goods is known as chattel paper.

"The chattel paper required the payment for the goods to be made within 30 days."

Codicil – As it relates to wills, a codicil is an attachment to a will that adds to or changes (modifies) the will in some way.

"A codicil to the will added their newly born daughter as a beneficiary."

Consideration – is what is given in value to induce someone to enter into a contract. Consideration examples are: property, money, services, etc.

"The consideration that the buyer of the land offered was a down payment in the amount of $35,000."

Contempt of court – are actions which hinder the execution of court orders and display disrespect of court authority.

"Because he repeatedly ignored the court orders, the judge declared that he was in contempt of court and fined him $500."

Contract – A contract (an agreement between parties) can be oral or written. For there to be a contract, there must be legal consideration to enter into the contract.

"The contractor and the homeowner signed a <u>contract</u> for the addition of a room to the house."

Conveyance – The instrument which creates, assigns, transfers, or surrenders an interest in real property is called a conveyance.

"They finalized the <u>conveyance</u> of the property on June 10, 2023."

Deponent – Deponent means the same as affiant. A deponent (affiant) is a person who signs the deposition and makes an oath to a written statement.

"The notary asked the <u>deponent</u> to sign the deposition."

Deposition – A deposition is testimony taken before an authorized official (such as a notary public). It is taken out of court with the intention of using it at a hearing or trial.

"The <u>deposition</u> on the auto accident case was held in a courtroom."

Duress – Duress means exercising unlawful constraint on a person with the intention of forcing him to do certain acts which may be against the person's will.

"He contested the contract because he said he was forced to sign it under <u>duress</u>."

Encumbrance – As it relates to real property, an encumbrance is a legal liability that attaches to property but does not prohibit passing the title to the property.

"The property had an <u>encumbrance</u> of taxes due in the amount of $12,000."

Escrow – is depositing an instrument with a person who on the occurrence of an event must give the instrument to a designated person. Escrow is often used during the sale of a building.

"The buyer and seller agreed that the down payment would be held in <u>escrow</u> by the lawyer until the closing of the house."

Executor – is a person designated (named) in a will to carry out the instructions of the deceased that are listed in the will.

"In the will, the grandfather named his grandson to be the <u>executor</u> of his estate because he knew that the grandson was intelligent and very competent in legal matters."

Ex Parte (one sided) – A court proceeding is ex parte (one sided) when it is conducted with only one of the parties being present (plaintiff or defendant).

"Because the defendant was absent, the judge decided to proceed <u>ex-parte</u> and render a default judgment."

Felony – Generally, an offense for which a sentence of imprisonment of more than a year (or death) may be imposed.

"<u>Felonies</u> are the most serious offenses."

Guardian – A guardian is a person in charge of another person's property or person (usually relates to guardians of minors).

"Because the person could not handle his own affairs, the court appointed a guardian."

Judgment – A judgment declares the rights of individuals, including that one party owes money to another and specifying the amount owed. Judgments may be final or temporary.

"The judge ordered a judgment in favor of the seller for the full amount that was still unpaid."

Jurat – A jurat is the section of an affidavit which contains the certification of the notary public that the document was sworn to in front of the notary public.

"The notary explained to the person that the jurat was at the end of the document."

Lease – A lease is a contract regarding the right to the possession of real property (land or buildings). It is made for consideration (rent, lease payments) and transfers the right to possession of real property for a period of time.

"The tenant had a two-year lease and an option to renew."

Lien – A lien is the attachment of a legal claim on property until the debt on the property is satisfied.

"The property had a tax lien for unpaid taxes."

Litigation – is the process of pursuing a lawsuit.

"The contract dispute was resolved by litigation that lasted two years."

Misdemeanor – an offense that is less serious than a felony and is punishable by a sentence of imprisonment up to and including a year.

"A misdemeanor is an offense that is lesser than a felony."

Mortgage on real property – A written instrument that is used to create a lien on real property until the debt is paid.

"The mortgage on the real property was for 30 years."

Oath – An oath or affirmation is a verbal pledge of the truth of a statement.

"The witness swore an oath to answer truthfully."

Plaintiff – A plaintiff is the party who starts a civil lawsuit.

"The landlord was the party who started the case and is referred to as the plaintiff."

Power of attorney – is a statement in writing by a person which gives another person the legal power to act for him.

"Because she would be in a recovery facility for one month, she gave her son a power of attorney to act on behalf of her in all financial matters."

Proof – as it relates to the witnessing of the execution of instruments, means the formal declaration of the witness that he witnessed the execution of the instrument. The witness must state his residence and that he knew the person signing the instrument.

"The notary took the proof of the execution of the document by examining the witness who had witnessed the execution of the document."

Protest – written statement by a notary that a promissory note or bill of exchange was presented for acceptance or payment was refused.

"A protest of a note is documented by the written statement of a notary that a promissory note or bill of exchange was presented for acceptance or payment was refused."

Statute – is a law that was created by the legislature.

"The statute specified the fee for the filing of the permit."

Statute of frauds – A law that states that certain contracts must be in writing to be enforceable. Other contracts (if partially completed) may also be enforceable.

"The auto dealer informed him that according to the statute of frauds, the auto purchase had to be in writing to be enforceable because it was for a contract for more than $500."

Statute of limitations - law which prescribe the time during which a civil action or criminal prosecution must be commenced.

"Although the contract had been signed four years ago, he knew that he could start a breach of contract action because it was still within the six-year statute of limitations period."

Subordination clause – A clause in an agreement (contract) which allows a future mortgage to take priority over an existing mortgage.

"In order to obtain a higher interest rate on the small mortgage, the lender agreed to a subordination clause in the mortgage which allowed a mortgage placed in the future to take priority over this mortgage."

Swear – a mode of oath administration authorized by law.

"In most states, a person can swear or affirm as to the truthfulness of a statement."

Venue – geographical area where acknowledgment or is taken by notary (Example: County of Fresno).

"The venue of a case involving real property is usually the geographical area where the land is located."

Will – the instrument in which a person sets forth his wishes relating to the disposition of his property after his death.

"Although she was still young, she had her lawyer prepare a will so that it would be clear how she wanted her property to be disposed in the event of her death."

The following 5 pages contain selected fees and penalties relating to notaries public. Please note that these lists are summaries and provided for quick memorization. For complete current fees and penalties, please refer to the official codes, statutes, and publications.

NOTARY FEES*
(Maximum fees a notary can charge)

Section	Fee Description	Maximum Fee
CGC 8211	Acknowledgments (per signature)	$15
CGC 8211	Jurats (per signature)	$15
CGC 8211	Certified copy of Power of Attorney Probate Code Section 4307	$15
CGC 8211	Deposition-all services	$30 + $7 for each oath to a witness and $7 for the certificate
CGC 8211	Oaths and Affirmations	$15 per person
	Voting materials signatures on vote by mail ballot, ID envelopes etc.	$0
	Immigration consultant forms data entering	$15 per individual for each set of forms
	Veteran's Benefit forms	$0
CGC 8206(c)	Copy of journal entry	$.30 per page

* Please refer to current law for any updated fees.

BOND TO BECOME A NOTARY

(CGC 8212)
The amount of the official notary public surety bond to be filed with the county clerk's office is $15,000

NOTARIAL FEES SHALL NOT BE CHARGED FOR THE FOLLOWING

CGC 8203.6: **NO** notarial fee can be charged by a notary appointed to a military or naval reservation, as per 8203.1.

Elections Code 8080: **NO** notarial fee can be charged for verifying a nomination document or circular's affidavit.

CGC 6106: **NO** notarial fee can be charged by a notary working for a public entity for an application, affidavit, or voucher used to secure a pension.

CGC 6107: **NO** notarial fee can be charged to a US military veteran for a claim for veteran's benefits, including an allotment, insurance, allowance, compensation, or for the pension application itself.

CGC 8211(d) **NO** notarial fee can be charged to notarize signatures on voting materials, including on "vote by mail ballot identification envelopes."

FINANCIAL PENALTIES FOR NOTARY OFFENSES

PENALTY NOT EXCEEDING $500

Willful failure to notify the Secretary of State of a change of address. (CGC 8213.5)

Willful failure to notify the Secretary of State of a change of a name. (CGC 8213.6)

PENALTY NOT EXCEEDING $750

Charging more than the maximum fees prescribed. (CGC 8214.1 (h))

Failure to complete the acknowledgment at the time the notary's signature and seal are affixed to the document. (CGC 8214.1 (j))

Failure to administer the oath or affirmation as required by paragraph (3) of subdivision (a) of Section 8205. (CGC 8214.1 (k))

PENALTY NOT EXCEEDING $1,000

Providing notary public education in violation of the regulations adopted by the Secretary of State for approved vendors, ($1,000) for each violation. Restitution may also be ordered. (CGC 8201.2)

PENALTY NOT EXCEEDING $1,500

(CGC 8207.4) Willful violation of any part of:
Section 8207.1 - using the notary public identification number
Section 8207.2 - notary seal or stamp manufacture, duplication, etc.
Section 8207.3 - lost or misplaced seal, etc.

Use of false or misleading advertising where the notary public has represented that the notary public has duties, rights, or privileges that he does not possess by law. (CGC 8214.1(f))

Commission of any act involving dishonesty, fraud, or deceit with the intent to substantially benefit the notary public or another, or substantially injure another. (CGC 8214.1(i))

Execution of any certificate as a notary public containing a statement known to the notary public to be false. (CGC 8214.1(l))

Violation of Section CGC 8223. Illegal advertising regarding immigration services)

Advertising in language other than English; posting of notice relating to legal advice and fees; translation of "notary public" into Spanish. (CGC 8214.1(o))

PENALTY NOT EXCEEDING $2500

Willful failure to provide access to the sequential journal of notarial acts when legally requested by a peace officer. (CGC 8214.21)

Failure to obtain a required thumbprint from a party signing a document. (CGC 8214.23(a))

PENALTY NOT EXCEEDING $10,000

Willfully stating as true any material fact known to be false. (Civil Code section 1189(a)(2))

Failing to obtain the satisfactory evidence required. (Civil Code 1185)

PENALTY NOT EXCEEDING $75,000

"Every person who files any false or forged document or instrument with the county recorder which affects title to, places an encumbrance on, or places an interest secured by a mortgage or deed of trust on, real property consisting of a single-family residence containing not more than four dwelling units, with knowledge that the document is false or forged, is punishable, in addition to any other punishment, by a fine not exceeding seventy-five thousand dollars ($75,000)." (Penal Code 115.5)

QUESTIONS PRACTICE

The following pages help you to reinforce your understanding by providing two types of questions:

1. "Quick questions" (6 on a page) and

2. "Multiple Choice Questions" (4 on a page)

We suggest that you do not continue to the multiple-choice questions until you have mastered the Quick Questions.

When you think you are ready, take each of the Practice Exams.

PLEASE NOTE

Whenever you answer a question incorrectly, review that section of law.

Also, make sure you are comfortable with all the legal terms. They will help you to understand and become comfortable with the law, both for the exam and later during your notary public career.

"Always bear in mind that your own resolution to succeed is more important than any other thing."

- Abraham Lincoln

QUESTIONS

Which arrests and convictions must an applicant for notary disclose?

T/F? An applicant may be disqualified for conviction of a disqualifying lesser offense.

Term of office for a notary starts with the starting date as stated in the commission and is ___ years long.

To serve as notary, a person must file with the clerk of county (within 30 days of the commission start date) both of the following:
1) oath of office, and
2) _____.

The power of a notary to act in an area (jurisdictional limit) is limited to which California counties?

A notary bond (from a surety insurer and required to be filed) must be in the sum of $_____.

ANSWERS

An applicant for notary must disclose the following:
1. arrests for which a **trial** is pending, and
2. all felony convictions and other lesser offenses (CGC 8214.1)

TRUE. An applicant may be disqualified for conviction of a disqualifying lesser offense. (CGC 8214.1)

Term of office for a notary public starts with the starting date as stated in the commission and is **FOUR (4)** years long. (CGC 8204)

To serve as notary public, a person must file with the clerk of county (within 30 days of the commission start date) both of the following:
1) oath of office, and 2) **a $15,000 bond.** (CGC 8212)

The power of a notary to act (jurisdiction) is in ALL California counties. (He may act in any county in California.) (CGC 8200)

A notary bond (from a surety insurer and required to be filed) must be in the sum of **$15,000.** (CGC 8212)

QUESTIONS

T/F? The notary public journal must always be kept in a secure place that is always under the control of the notary.

What is a possible penalty if a notary fails to secure his journal?

Journal entries must be made when the notarial act is done and must be recorded _____.

If a notary intentionally (willfully) doesn't properly maintain his journal, he is guilty of _____.

May a member of the public request the original of a journal entry?

How much can a notary charge per photocopy page for requests for copies of journal entries? (CGC 8206(c))

ANSWERS

TRUE. The notary public journal must always be kept in a secure place that is always under the control of the notary. (CGC 8206(a)(1))

If a notary fails to secure his journal, his notary public commission may be **suspended or revoked AND civil and criminal penalties may be imposed.** (CGC 8214.1(o), 8214.15(b), and 8228.1)

Journal entries must be made when the notarial act is done and must be recorded **sequentially.** (CGC 8206(a)(1))

If a notary intentionally (willfully) doesn't properly maintain his journal, he is guilty of a **misdemeanor**. (CGC 8206(a) and 8228.1(a))

NO. A member of the public may only request **a photocopy** of a journal entry. (CGC 8206(c))

The notary can charge **30 cents ($.30)** per photocopy page. (CGC 8206(c))

QUESTIONS

What is the title of the state official of California who appoints notaries in California?

For an applicant to be eligible for a notary public appointment, must he be a resident of the state of California?

T/F? The Secretary of State may appoint notaries for the military reservations in California.

A person applying for notary is required to complete a course (in a satisfactory manner) approved by the California Secretary of State that is ___ hours long.

An exception to the 6-hour rule: an applicant may complete a ___ hour refresher course if he meets the following two conditions: (1) he currently holds an active notary public commission AND (2) he has already completed a 6-hour course as part of a previous application.

T/F? A person to be appointed a notary must be a legal resident of California at the time of application.

ANSWERS

California **Secretary of State.** (CGC 8200)

Yes, unless he is appointed to serve on a military or naval reservation). **The applicant must also be at least 18 years old.** (CGC 8201)

TRUE. This is an important exception to the general rule that requires a California notary public to be a resident of California. (CGC 8203.1)

A person applying for notary is required to complete a course (in a satisfactory manner) approved by the California Secretary of State that is **6 (SIX)** hours long. (CGC 8201(a)(3))

An exception to the 6-hour rule: an applicant may complete a **3-hour** refresher course if he meets the following two conditions: (1) he currently holds an active notary public commission AND (2) he has already completed a 6-hour course as part of a previous application. (CGC 8201(b)(2))

FALSE. A person to be appointed a notary must be a legal resident of California at the time of. Appointment. CGC 8201(a)(1))

QUESTIONS

If a notary willfully (intentionally) fails to deliver his journal and other files to the county clerk, he is guilty of a _____ offense.

The seal used by a notary must be purchased from a company (vendor) authorized by who?

T/F? One of the requirements that a notary seal must meet is that it must be "photographically reproducible."

The notary seal may be _____ or rectangular.

From whom can a notary purchase a seal?

Which California official issues certificates which authorize a notary to purchase an official notary public seal?

ANSWERS

If a notary willfully (intentionally) fails to deliver his journal and other files to the county clerk, he is guilty of a **misdemeanor** offense. (CGC 8209(a))

The seal used by a notary must be purchased from a company (vendor) authorized by the **Secretary of State**. (CGC 8207, 8207.2, and 8207.3)

TRUE. Must also contain: 1. State Seal; 2. words "Notary Public"; 3. name of notary; 4. expiration date of commission; 5. county where oath and bond are filed; 6, commission number; 7. sequential ID number of the manufacturer/vendor. (CGC 8207)

The notary seal may be **circular** or rectangular.
1. **circular** (not more than 2 inches in diameter), or
2. **rectangular** (not more than 1-inch width by 2&½ inches length). (CGC 8207)

The seal may be purchased only from a manufacturer or vendor that is authorized by the Secretary of State. (CGC 8207.2 and 8207.3)

The California Secretary of State. The original certificate of authorization must be used – and **NOT** a copy. (CGC 8207.2 and 8207.3)

QUESTIONS

T/F? A notary who is negligent may be personally liable for damages, costs, and attorney's fees.

T/F? An employee of a California state, city or county public school district agency, or public agency may be appointed to serve as a notary for that entity.

T/F? A person appointed as a notary for a public entity may only act as a notary for that public entity.

T/F? If the employee notary (of a public employer) resigns or is terminated, this is considered the same as a resignation of the commission of the notary.

A person appointed as a notary to serve on a military reservation must be a _____ citizen.

T/F? A person appointed a notary to serve on a military reservation may perform his duties only on the military reservation where he is appointed.

ANSWERS

TRUE. A notary who is negligent may be personally liable for damages, costs, and attorney's fees. (Even if the amount is greater than his insurance bond limits.) (CGC 8214)

TRUE. An employee of a California state, city or county public school district agency, or public agency may be appointed to serve as a notary for that entity.(CGC 8202.5)

TRUE. A person appointed as a notary for a public entity may only act as a notary for that entity. (CGC 8202.5)

TRUE. If the employee notary (of a public employer) resigns or is terminated, this is considered the same as a resignation of the commission of the notary. (CGC 8209)

A person appointed as a notary to serve on a military reservation must be a **US CITIZEN**. However, he does **NOT** have to be a California resident. (CGC 8203.1)

TRUE. A person appointed a notary to serve on a military reservation may perform his duties only on the military reservation where he is appointed. (He cannot collect any fees.) (CGC 8203.2 and 8203.6)

QUESTIONS

T/F? A notary applicant who completed a SIX (6) hour course in the last TWO (2) years doesn't have to take a THREE (3) hour refresher course.

T/F? Generally, notary applicants do not have to pass the written examination to be appointed.

If a notary applicant passes the written examination, he must provide his fingerprints to the Department of Justice of California within _____ year(s) to complete his background check.

If an applicant has been convicted of a crime, he (MAY? / MUST?) be denied appointment.

A _____ (or an offense not compatible with notary public duties) is considered a "disqualifying crime."

What is the title of the official responsible for determining whether an applicant has the required qualities to be a notary (honesty, credibility, truthfulness, and integrity)?

ANSWERS

TRUE. A notary public applicant who completed a SIX (6) hour course in the last TWO (2) years doesn't have to take a THREE (3) hour refresher course. (CGC 8201(a)(3))

FALSE. All applicants for appointment must pass the examination. (CGC 8201(a)(4))

If a notary applicant passes the written examination, he must provide his fingerprints to the Department of Justice of California within **1 (ONE YEAR)** to complete his background check. (CGC 8201.1(a))

If an applicant has been convicted of a crime, he **MAY** be denied appointment. (CGC 8214.1(b))

A **felony** (or an offense not compatible with notary public duties) is considered a "disqualifying crime." (CGC 8214.1(b))

California Secretary of State." (CGC 8201.1(a))

QUESTIONS

If a notary completes a certificate of acknowledgment that he knows is false, he may be liable for civil penalties and _____ action. (CGC 8214.15)

A notary is guilty of forgery if he issues an acknowledgment that he knows is _____.

Forgery is punishable by imprisonment for not more than _____ year(s).

What is the name of the certificate where a person swears (or affirms) that the contents of the document are true and correct?

A(n) _____ is a document which contains statements that have been sworn or affirmed by the signer to be true and correct.

T/F? For a notary to complete a jurat, he must certify that the signer personally appeared before him. The appearance must have been on the date and in the county indicated.

ANSWERS

If a notary completes a certificate of acknowledgment that he knows is false, he may be liable for civil penalties and **administrative** action. (CGC 8214.15)

A notary is guilty of forgery if he issues an acknowledgment that he knows is **false**. (California Penal Code 470(d))

Forgery is punishable by imprisonment for not more than **one** year. (California Penal Code 473)

The name is a **jurat.** (CGC 8202)

An **affidavit** is a document which contains statements that have been sworn or affirmed by the signer to be true and correct. (Legal Term)

TRUE. For a notary to complete a jurat, he must certify that the signer personally appeared before him. The appearance must have been on the date and in the county indicated. (CGC 8202(a))

QUESTIONS

T/F? A notary who performs notarial services for an employer must allow the employer to inspect journal entries without the notary being present.

T/F? If the employer requests, the notary (employee) must provide certified copies of journal entries made in the course of the employer's business.

T/F? If a notary is served with a <u>subpoena duces tecum</u> (a subpoena for the production of records) or with any other valid court order, he must provide the journal for examination and copying (while in his presence).

T/F? The journal of the notary is his exclusive property.

The notary is prohibited from allowing his employer to handle the journal without the notary being present.

A notary must surrender his journal without delay to a peace officer investigating a crime and has reasonable cause to believe the journal has _____ of a criminal offense.

ANSWERS

FALSE. The notary **MUST** be present. (CGC 8206(d))

FALSE. The notary must provide plain copies **(NOT certified copies)** of the journal entries. (CGC 8206(d))

TRUE. Also, if certified copies are requested, the notary must certify the copies. (CGC 8206(e))

TRUE. He is prohibited from surrendering it to anyone unless he is required to do so by any of the following:
1) by law, or
2) by a peace officer after a legal request, or
3) by a county clerk. (CGC 8206(d))

TRUE. The notary is prohibited from allowing his employer to handle the journal without the notary being present. (CGC 8206(d))

A notary must surrender his journal without delay to a peace officer investigating a crime and has reasonable cause to believe the journal has **evidence** of a criminal offense. (CGC 8206(d))

QUESTIONS

T/F? Acceptable ID is a qualifying driver's license issued by any US state or by a Canadian or Mexican agency authorized to issue licenses (IF ID has photo, description of person, signature, and ID number).

T/F? Acceptable ID is a qualifying ID card issued by any other US state. (IF ID has photo, description of person, signature, and ID number.).

T/F? Acceptable ID is all ID cards issued by a Canadian or Mexican public agency.

T/F? Acceptable ID is all US military identification cards.

T/F? Acceptable ID is an employee ID issued by an agency of a California city, a California county, or the State of California (with required information).

The signer's identity (can / cannot) be established by the oath of a single credible witness who personally knows the signer.

ANSWERS

TRUE. Acceptable ID is a qualifying driver's license issued by any US state or by a Canadian or Mexican agency authorized to issue licenses. (California Civil Code 1185(b)(4))

TRUE. Acceptable ID is a qualifying ID card issued by any another US state. (California Civil Code 1185(b)(4))

FALSE. ID card issued by a Canadian or Mexican public agency is **NOT** acceptable. (California Civil Code 1185(b)(4)) **UNLESS** ID has photo, description of person, signature, and ID number.

FALSE. All US military identification cards are not acceptable because some do not have the required information. (California Civil Code 1185(b)(4))

TRUE. Acceptable ID is an employee ID issued by an agency of a California city, a California county, or the State of California. (California Civil Code 1185(b)(4))

The signer's identity **CAN** be established this way **IF** the notary knows the credible witness personally (and proper ID of credible witness is provided). (California Civil Code 1185(b)(1))

QUESTIONS

Reasons for refusal to appoint or punish a notary public include forgery or grand _____.

Reasons for refusal to appoint or punish a notary public include obtaining personal information of another person to be used for _____ purposes.

Reasons for refusal to appoint or punish a notary public include refusal to supply the sequential journal after a proper request by a _____ officer.

Civil Penalty: up to and including $750 or $1,500?
Dishonesty, fraud, deceit.

Civil Penalty: up to and including $750 or $1,500?
Misleading advertising by the notary public.

Civil Penalty: up to and including $750 or $1,500?
Charging more than the maximum fees for notarial services.

ANSWERS

Reasons for refusal to appoint or punish a notary public include forgery or grand **theft**. (CGC 8214.4)

Reasons for refusal to appoint or punish a notary public include obtaining personal information of another person to be used for **criminal** purposes. (CGC 8214.4)

Reasons for refusal to appoint or punish a notary public include refusal to supply the sequential journal after a proper request by a **peace** officer. (CGC 8214.4)

Civil Penalty: up to and including $750 or $1,500? Dishonesty, fraud, deceit: up to and including **$1,500**. (CGC 8214.15)

Civil Penalty: Misleading advertising by the notary public: up to and including **$1,500**. (CGC 8214.15)

Civil Penalty: Charging more than the maximum fees for notarial services: up to and including **$750**. (CGC 8214.15)

QUESTIONS

When a notary surrenders his journal to a peace officer, he must obtain a receipt. The notary is also required to notify the Secretary of State within _____ days by certified mail.

Notification of the surrender of a journal to a peace officer must include a copy of the _____ provided by the peace officer.

If a notary journal is stolen, the notary must without delay notify the _____ by:
1) certified mail, or
2) registered mail.

If the journal of a notary is no longer available, the notary must acquire _____.

After the resignation or removal of a notary, the notary journal and all other relevant records must be given to the _____ where the notary public's oath is on file.

If a notary who has applied for reappointment is not reappointed within ___ days after the end of his commission, he must surrender his journal and all other relevant records to the county clerk.

ANSWERS

When a notary surrenders his journal to a peace officer, he must obtain a receipt. The notary is also required to notify the Secretary of State within **10 days** by certified mail. (CGC 8206(d))

Notification of the surrender of a journal to a peace officer must include a copy of the **receipt** provided by the peace officer. (CGC 8206(d))

If a notary journal is stolen, the notary must without delay notify the **Secretary of State** by:
1) certified mail, or
2) registered mail.
(CGC 8206(b))

If the journal of a notary is no longer available, the notary must acquire **a new journal.** (CGC 8206(d))

After the resignation or removal of a notary, the notary journal and all other relevant records must be given to the **clerk of county** where the notary public's oath is on file. (CGC 8209(a))

If a notary who has applied for reappointment is not reappointed within **30 days** after the end of his commission, he must surrender his journal and all other relevant records to the county clerk. (CGC 8209(a))

QUESTIONS

A change of address by a notary can be reported by letter or by the _____ at www.sos.ca.gov/notary.

T/F? The required fee to submit an address change form or address change letter is $15.00.

T/F? If a notary changes his business address to a different county, the notary may (if he wishes) file a new oath and bond or may file a new oath and copy of original bond, in the county of the new business.

T/F? A name change form must be submitted to the Secretary of State if a notary changes his name.

If a notary receives an amended commission, he must file with the county clerk of the county where his place of business is located (within 30 days of the date of issuance of the amended commission): 1) a new oath of office and 2) amendment to _____.

How many days does a notary have to answer a written request for information from the California Secretary of State?

ANSWERS

A change of address by a notary can be reported by letter or by the **change of address form** at www.sos.ca.gov/notary (the website of the Secretary of State). (CGC 8213)

FALSE. There is **NO FEE** to submit an address change form or address change letter. (CGC 8213)

TRUE. If a notary changes his business address to a different county, the notary may (if he wishes) file a new oath and bond or may file a new oath and copy of original bond, in the county of the new business. (CGC 8213 (b))

TRUE. A name change form must be submitted to the Secretary of State. However, the commission number and commission expiration date **will remain the same**. (CGC 8213.6)

If a notary receives an amended commission, he must file with the county clerk of the county where his place of business is located (within 30 days of the date of issuance of the amended commission): 1) a new oath of office and 2) amendment to **the bond.** (CGC 8213(c))

A notary public must answer within **30 days** after he receives the request. (CGC 8205(b)(2))

QUESTIONS

An agreement between a notary and a private employer (MAY? or SHALL NOT?) state that notary fees collected are required to be turned over to the employer.

If an employer pays the costs of notarial duties (bond, filing fees, etc.,) the employer (may? / may not?) insist that the notary employee provide notary services only for transactions related to the business.

T/F? A notary public is responsible for following relevant California state law. He is prohibited from following a conflicting law, even if cited by his employer.

A person who influences a notary to do an improper act is guilty of a _____.

What kind of journal must the notary keep?

Who is authorized to have access to the notary journal without the notary being present?

ANSWERS

An agreement between a notary and a private employer **MAY** state that notary fees collected are required to be turned over to the employer. (CGC 8205(b)(2))

If an employer pays the costs of notarial duties (bond, filing fees, etc.,) the employer **MAY** insist that the notary employee provide notary services only for transactions related to the business. (CGC 8202.8)

TRUE. A notary public is responsible for following relevant California state law. He is prohibited from following a conflicting law, even if cited by his employer. (CGC 8225)

A person who influences a notary to do an improper act is guilty of a **misdemeanor**. (CGC 8225)

He must keep one active journal (with sequential entries and all required details of the notarial acts that he performs). (CGC 8206(a)(1))

No one is authorized to have access to the notary journal without the notary being present (including an employer). (CGC 8206(a)(1))

QUESTIONS

T/F? The notary seal must be:
1. kept in a secure area that is locked, and
2. the area must be under the exclusive control of the notary.

The notary seal is the property of the notary. Generally, it can't be surrendered to anyone, even an employer who paid for the seal. (CGC 8207) What is one exception to this rule?

When is a seal not required to carry out a notarial duty?

Documents that are acknowledged may be recorded by the county clerk. Because of this, the seal must be _____.

T/F? If a seal is lost, destroyed, etc., that fact must be reported to the Secretary of State by:
1. mail, or
2. by delivery of a written notice.

The notary (or his representative) must destroy the seal upon: 1. resignation; 2. termination; 3. revocation of the notary commission; or 4. _____ of the notary.

ANSWERS

TRUE. The notary seal must be:
1. kept in a secure area that is locked, and
2. the area must be under the exclusive control of the notary. (CGC 8228)

The exception is when a seal is surrendered on demand of **a court order**. (CGC 8207)

A seal is **NOT** required for acknowledgments on California subdivision maps. (CGC 66436 (c))

Documents that are acknowledged may be recorded by the county clerk. Because of this, the seal must be **legible.** (CGC 8207)

TRUE. The California Secretary of State will then, upon request, issue within 5 days a new certificate of authorization to purchase a seal. (CGC 8207.3(e))

The notary or his representative must destroy the seal upon: 1. resignation; 2. termination; 3. revocation of the notary commission; or 4. **death** of the notary. (CGC 8207)

QUESTIONS

T/F? In a certificate of acknowledgment, the notary certifies that the signer did not appear before the notary.

T/F? In a certificate of acknowledgment, the notary certifies that he 1) verified the identity of the signer, and that 2) the signer acknowledged signing.

Can a notary take an acknowledgment of a document if he concludes that the document is incomplete?

The type of evidence that a notary uses to confirm the identity of the signer is called _____.

When a notary takes an acknowledgment, does the person have to sign the document in the presence of the notary?

(For an acknowledgment)
If there is one credible witness, the witness must: 1) sign the journal, OR 2) the notary must record the details of the ID of the _____.

ANSWERS

FALSE. In a certificate of acknowledgment, the notary certifies that the signer **DID APPEAR** before the notary. (CGC 1189)

TRUE. In a certificate of acknowledgment, the notary certifies that he 1) verified the identity of the signer, and that 2) the signer acknowledged signing. (Civil Code 1189)

NO. A notary **CANNOT** take an acknowledgment of a document if he concludes that the document is incomplete. (CGC 8205(a)(2))

The type of evidence that a notary uses to confirm the identity of the signer is called "**satisfactory evidence**". (Civil Code 1185)

NO. When a notary takes an acknowledgment, the person does NOT have to sign the document in the presence of the notary. He can acknowledge that he signed the document. (California Civil Code 1189)

(For an acknowledgment)
If there is one credible witness, the witness must: 1) sign the journal, OR 2) the notary must record the details of the ID of the **credible witness**. (CGC 8206(a)(2)(D))

QUESTIONS

The only title that a notary public can use is: "_____."

A notary can only perform notarial acts described in _____ law.

When a notary "notarizes a document," he is notarizing the _____ of the person signing the document.

If a notary has a financial interest in the document to be notarized, is he allowed to notarize his own signature?

Before a notary can notarize the signature on a document, he must inspect the document and determine that the document is _____. (CGC 8205)

If a notary knows that certain information should be included in a document, and that information is not there, the notary must _____.

ANSWERS

The notary public can only use the official title "**notary public.**" (CGC 8207)

A notary can only perform notarial acts described in **California** law. (CGC 8202, 8205 and 8207; California Civil Code 1189))

When a notary "notarizes a document," he is notarizing the **signature** of the person signing the document. (CGC 8202, 8205, 8207)

NO. If a notary has a financial interest, he **CANNOT** notarize his own signature. (CGC 8224 and 8224.1)

Before a notary can notarize the signature on a document, he must inspect the document and determine that the document is **complete**. (CGC 8205)

If a notary knows that certain information should be included in a document, and that information is not there, the notary must **refuse to notarize the document.** (CGC 8205(a)(2))

QUESTIONS

If a document is in Spanish, German, French, etc., can a notary notarize a signature in that document?

Is it a requirement that a notary be able to communicate with his customer?

If a notary is not able to identify the type of foreign language document being notarized, what entry does he make in the journal as to the "type of document"?

The notarial certificate of a document in a foreign language must be written in which language?

The notary must confirm the _____ of the person whose signature is on the document before he can notarize the signature.

T/F? "Satisfactory evidence" is evidence used to establish the identity of the signer.

ANSWERS

YES. If a document is in a foreign language, a notary **CAN** notarize a signature in that document. (California Civil Code 1189 and 1195; CGC 8202, 8205 and 8206)

YES. An interpreter must not be used. The customer should be referred to a notary who speaks the customer's language. (California Civil Code 189, 1195; CGC 8202, 8205, 8206)

He must make an entry such as **"a document in a foreign language."** (California Civil Code 189 and 1195; CGC 8202, 8205 and 8206)

The notarial certificate **must be written in English.** (California Civil Code 1188, 1189 and 1195; CGC 8202)

The notary must confirm the **identity** of the person whose signature is on the document before he can notarize the signature. (California Civil Code 1185(a) and (b), and 1189; CGC 8202)

TRUE. "Satisfactory evidence" includes: 1) the oath of 1 credible witness, 2) the oaths of 2 credible witnesses, and 3) proper identification documents. (California Civil Code 1185(b))

QUESTIONS

If a notary personally knows a signer, is that sufficient to establish the identity of the signer?

A requirement of ID documents is that they must be current or issued within the previous _____ years. (California Civil Code 1185(b)(3))

T/F? A passport issued by the U.S. does not have to have the description of the person to be acceptable ID.

T/F? For an inmate ID card to be valid, the inmate doesn't have to be in custody of the issuing state or local sheriff's department detention facility.

ID's listed as "reasonable evidence" must have: the serial number or other identifying number, a photograph and description of the person, and the _____ of the person.

T/F? Acceptable ID is a Passport issued by any foreign government.

ANSWERS

NO. It not sufficient. (California Civil Code 1185(b))

A requirement of ID documents is that they must be current or issued within the previous **5 years**. (California Civil Code 1185(b)(3))

TRUE. A passport issued by the U.S. does not have to have the description of the person to be acceptable ID. (California Civil Code 1185(b)(3))

FALSE. For an inmate ID card to be valid, the inmate **HAS TO BE IN CUSTODY** of the issuing state or local sheriff's department detention facility. (California Civil Code 1185(b)(3))

ID's listed in California Civil Code 1185(b)(4)) are acceptable must have: the serial number or other identifying number, a photograph and description of the person, and the **signature** of the person.

FALSE. To be acceptable, a foreign passport must have been stamped by the U.S. Immigration or Naturalization Service or the U.S. Citizenship and Immigration Service. (California Civil Code 1185(b)(4))

QUESTIONS

Generally, can a notary public perform a marriage?

The statutory fees for notarial services are the MINIMUM? or MAXIMUM? fees allowed?

If the notary doesn't charge a fee for a service, he must write in his journal "_____" to indicate no fee was charged.

MAXIMUM ALLOWABLE FEES
Acknowledgment or proof of a deed (or other instrument, including the seal and writing the certificate) $___ for each signature acknowledged.

MAXIMUM ALLOWABLE FEES
Administering an oath or affirmation to one person and executing the jurat, including the seal, $___.

MAXIMUM ALLOWABLE FEES
For services in connection with the taking of a deposition, $___, and an additional $___ for administering the oath to the witness and $___ for the certificate to the deposition.

ANSWERS

Generally, a notary public **CANNOT** perform a marriage **UNLESS** he is authorized by California law (Example: priest, minister, or rabbi. (California Family Code 400 – 402)

The statutory fees for notarial services are the **MAXIMUM** fees allowed. (Notary handbook)

If the notary doesn't charge a fee for a service, he must write in his journal "**zero**" to indicate no fee was charged. (CGC 8206(a))

MAXIMUM ALLOWABLE FEES
Acknowledgment or proof of a deed (or other instrument, including the seal and writing the certificate) **$15** for each signature acknowledged. (CGC 8211)

MAXIMUM ALLOWABLE FEES
Administering an oath or affirmation to one person and executing the jurat, including the seal, **$15.** (CGC 8211)

MAXIMUM ALLOWABLE FEES For services in connection with the taking of a deposition, **$30**, and an additional **$7** for administering the oath to the witness and **$7** for the certificate to the deposition. (CGC 8211)

QUESTIONS

A notary public must file (with the county clerk) his 1) oath of office, AND 2) a $15,000 surety bond. Both must be filed within ___ days of the start date in the notary commission.

The notary commission becomes invalid if 1) oath and 2) bond are not filed with the county clerk within ___ days of the notary public start date (commission date).

In what county or counties must the notary file his oath and bond?

T/F? The notary commission is NOT valid if both the oath and bond are not filed within 30 days of the start date in the commission. Excuses such as mail delays or processing delays do not change this requirement.

A county clerk employee can administer the notary public oath and observe the notary signing the oath. In such a case, the oath and bond are filed _____.

If a notary changes his business address or residence address, he must inform the Secretary of State by <u>certified</u> mail within ___ days.

ANSWERS

A notary public must file (with the county clerk) his 1) oath of office, AND 2) a $15,000 surety bond. Both must be filed within **30 (THIRTY)** days of the start date in the notary commission. (CGC 8213.)

A notary public must file (with the county clerk) his 1) oath of office, AND 2) a $15,000 surety bond. Both must be filed within **30 (THIRTY)** days of the commencement date stated by the Secretary of State. (CGC 8213)

Both the oath and bond must be filed with the county clerk where the **principal place of business of the notary** is located. (CGC 8213)

TRUE. Notary commission is NOT valid if both the oath and bond are not filed within **30 (THIRTY)** days of the start date in the commission. Excuses such as mail delays or processing delays do not change requirement. (CGC 8213)

A county clerk employee can administer the notary public oath and observe the notary signing the oath. In such a case, the oath and bond are filed **the same day**. (CGC 8213)

If a notary public changes his business address or residence address, he must inform the Secretary of State by <u>certified</u> mail within **THIRTY (30) DAYS**. (CGC 8213.5)

QUESTIONS

A notary is guilty of an infraction if he willfully (intentionally) doesn't notify the Secretary of State of his change of address. This infraction may be punished by a fine not exceeding _____.

T/F? A 1) business address, and 2) a residence address must be listed on the notary application.

T/F? On the notary application, the applicant must include the name of the business where he will perform any notarial services.

If there is not one address where the notary plans to perform a majority of his notarial services, the business address he lists must be where he plans to perform most of his notarial services, or the business address where he will receive _____.

T/F? A private commercial mailbox or post office box may not be listed as the 1) residence address, OR 2) the principal place of business.

T/F? A change to any of the addresses listed by the notary does not have to be reported to the Secretary of State.

ANSWERS

A notary is guilty of an infraction if he willfully (intentionally) doesn't notify the Secretary of State of his change of address. This infraction may be punished by a fine not exceeding **$500**. (CGC 8213.5)

TRUE. Also, the applicant **MAY** list a mailing address **that IS different** from other addresses provided. (CGC 8201.5 and 8213.5)

FALSE. The applicant must state in his application the name of the business only if he plans to **perform a majority** of his notarial services for it. (CGC 8201.5 and 8213.5)

If there is not one address where the notary plans to perform a majority of his notarial services, the business address he lists must be where he plans to perform most of his notarial services, or the business address where he will receive **mail related to his notary public commission.** (CGC 8201.5 and 8213.5.)

TRUE. Exception: A notary may do so **IF** he also provides the Secretary of State with the actual **physical street address** of his principal residence. (CGC 8213.5)

FALSE. Any address change **MUST** be reported to the Secretary of State. (CGC 8213)

QUESTIONS

(Jurat) The signer's identity may be established by the oaths or affirmations of one or _____ credible witnesses, or the signer may present "credible" ID as stated in California Civil Code 1185(b)(3) and (b)(4).

(Jurat) OATH:
"Do you solemnly swear or _____ that the contents of this document are the truth, the whole truth, and nothing but the truth, so help you God?"

(Jurat) AFFIRMATION:
"Do you solemnly swear or _____, under penalty of perjury, that the contents of this document are the truth, the whole truth, and nothing but the truth?"

T/F? A notary can certify copies of vital records (such as birth, marriage, and death certificates).

If a person, (the "principal"), has signed a document but can't appear in front of the notary, a "_____ witness" can appear to prove the principal signed the document. (California Code of Civil Procedure 1935)

A proof of execution by a subscribing witness (CAN? / CANNOT?) be used for documents relating to any power of attorney.

ANSWERS

(Jurat) The signer's identity may be established by the oaths or affirmations of one or **two** credible witnesses, or the signer may present "credible" ID as stated in California Civil Code 1185(b)(3) and (b)(4).

(Jurat) OATH:
"Do you solemnly swear or **affirm** that the contents of this document are the truth, the whole truth, and nothing but the truth, so help you God?" (California Code of Civil Procedure 2094(2); California Evidence Code 165)

(Jurat) AFFIRMATION:
"Do you solemnly swear or **affirm**, under penalty of perjury, that the contents of this document are the truth, the whole truth, and nothing but the truth?" (California Code of Civil Procedure 2094(2); California Evidence Code 165)

FALSE. A notary **CANNOT** certify copies of vital records. (CGC 8230)

If a person, (the "principal"), has signed a document but can't appear in front of the notary, a "**subscribing** witness" can appear to prove the principal signed the document. (California Code of Civil Procedure 1935.)

A proof of execution by a subscribing witness **CANNOT** be used for documents relating to any power of attorney. (California Government Code 2787; California Civil Code 1195(b)(1) and (2))

QUESTIONS

T/F? Notary applicants must list on their notary application all arrests for which trials are pending and all convictions.

T/F? Failure to perform correctly the duties or responsibilities of a notary is a reason for refusal to appoint or punish a notary public.

T/F? Omission or material misstatement in a notary application is a reason for refusal to appoint or punish a notary public.

T/F? A conviction for a felony and certain lesser included offenses is a reason for refusal to appoint or punish a notary public.

T/F? Revocation, suspension, restriction, or denial of a professional license based on misconduct or dishonesty are causes for refusal to appoint or punish a notary public.

False or misleading advertising includes when a notary advertises he has rights or privileges that he (does? / does not?) have.

ANSWERS

TRUE. Notary applicants must list on their notary application all arrests for which trials are pending and all convictions. (CGC 8201.1 and 8201.5)

TRUE. Failure to perform correctly the duties or responsibilities of a notary is a reason for refusal to appoint or punish a notary public. (CGC 8214.4)

TRUE. Omission or material misstatement in a notary application is a reason for refusal to appoint or punish a notary public. (CGC 8214.4)

TRUE. A conviction for a felony and certain lesser included offenses is a reason for refusal to appoint or punish a notary public. (CGC 8214.4)

TRUE. Revocation, suspension, restriction, or denial of a professional license based on misconduct or dishonesty are causes for refusal to appoint or punish a notary public. (CGC 8214.4)

False or misleading advertising includes when a notary advertises he has rights or privileges that he **DOES NOT** have. (CGC 8214.4)

QUESTIONS

In a journal entry for proof of execution by a subscribing witness, what would be a proper entry for "the type of notarial act performed"?

In a journal entry for proof of execution by a subscribing witness, what would be a journal entry for "the type of document"?

In a journal entry for proof of execution by a subscribing witness, what would be a journal entry for the "name of the subscribing witness"?

In a journal entry for proof of execution by a subscribing witness, what would be a journal entry for the "notarial act fee"?

Proof of execution by a subscribing witness:
The name of the county in the "venue statement" is the county where _____.

Proof of execution by a subscribing witness:
The day, month and year in the journal must be the date the subscribing personally appeared _____.

ANSWERS

The type of act would be a **"proof of execution by a subscribing witness."** (Notary Handbook)

The journal entry would be the title of the document as stated in the document. The title is usually found at the top of the page. (Notary Handbook)

IF the signature of the subscribing witness is included, then also include the name of the subscribing witness. (Notary Handbook)

The journal entry would be the amount of fee collected. (Notary Handbook)

Proof of execution by a subscribing witness:
The name of the county in the "venue statement" is the county where **the notarial act occurred**. (Notary Handbook)

Proof of execution by a subscribing witness:
The day, month and year in the journal must be the date the subscribing personally appeared **before the notary public.** (Notary Handbook)

QUESTIONS

Proof of execution by a subscribing witness:
In the journal, the name of the _____ (person who signed the document but didn't appear before the notary but told the subscribing witness that he signed the document) must be inserted.

Proof of execution by a subscribing witness:
A notary who completes this certificate verifies only the _____ of the person who signed the document (and NOT the document's accuracy, validity, or truthfulness).

Signature by Mark
If a person cannot write, he can make a "_____" (for example: "X").

Signature by Mark
If a person makes a mark, the witnesses must _____ the person when he makes the mark.

Signature by Mark
T/F? If there are two witnesses to the making of the mark, they are not required to be identified by the notary and are not required to sign the journal.

Certifying copies

T/F? A notary can certify powers of attorney.

ANSWERS

Proof of execution by a subscribing witness:
In the journal, the name of the **principal** (person who signed the document but didn't appear before the notary but told the subscribing witness that he signed the document) must be inserted. (Notary Handbook)

Proof of execution by a subscribing witness:
A notary who completes this certificate verifies only the **identity** of the person who signed the document (and NOT the document's accuracy, validity, or truthfulness). (Notary Handbook)

Signature by Mark
If a person cannot write, he can make a "Mark" (for example: "X", or "Y", or "ZZ", etc.). (California Civil Code 14)

Signature by Mark
If a person makes a mark, the witnesses must **observe** the person when he makes the mark. (Notary Handbook)

Signature by Mark
TRUE. If there are two witnesses to the making of the mark, they are not required to be identified by the notary and are not required to sign the journal. (Notary Handbook)

Certifying copies

TRUE. A notary can certify powers of attorney. (California Probate Code 4307; CGC 8205(a)(4))

QUESTIONS

Perjury is punishable by a term of imprisonment in a state jail for _____ years.

If a person is convicted of a _____, the court must revoke the notary commission and order the notary to surrender the notary seal to the court.

T/F? If a person is convicted of any crime relating to misconduct on the part of the notary, the court must revoke the notary commission and order the notary to surrender the notary seal to the court.

If a notary fails or refuses to deliver his notarial records to the county clerk within 30 days of resignation or removal from office, or within 30 days of commission expiration, the person is guilty of a _____.

A person who destroys, conceals, or defaces records belonging to a notary is guilty of a _____.

A person who influences a notary to do an improper notarial act is guilty of a _____.

ANSWERS

Perjury is punishable by a term of imprisonment in a state jail for **TWO, THREE, or FOUR** years. (California Penal Code 126)

If a person is convicted of a **felony**, the court must revoke the notary commission and order the notary to surrender the notary seal to the court. (CGC 8214.8)

TRUE. If a person is convicted of any crime relating to misconduct on the part of the notary, the court must revoke the notary commission and order the notary to surrender the notary seal to the court. (CGC 8214.8)

If a notary fails or refuses to deliver his notarial records to the county clerk within 30 days of resignation or removal from office, or within 30 days of commission expiration, the person is guilty of a **misdemeanor**. (CGC 8209(a))

A person who destroys, conceals, or defaces records belonging to a notary is guilty of a **MISDEMEANOR.** (CGC 8221)

A person who influences a notary to do an improper notarial act is guilty of a **misdemeanor**. (CGC 8225(a))

QUESTIONS

Certifying copies
Can a notary certify copies of birth, fetal, death, and marriage records?

Can a notary notarize the signature on a document which relates to citizenship or immigration?

Can a notary advise a person on immigration forms?

T/F? A notary public WHO IS ALSO a California registered immigration consultant CAN write on immigration forms the answers given to him by the client.

What is the amount that a notary who is also a registered immigration consultant can charge each person for completing a set of immigration papers?

T/F? A notary **is prohibited** from advertising that he is a notary if he also holds himself out to be an immigration consultant or specialist.

ANSWERS

Certifying copies
NO. A notary CANNOT certify such documents. They can be certified only by other legally empowered officials. (Notary Handbook)

YES. A notary CAN notarize the signature on a document which relates to citizenship or immigration. However, a notary CANNOT help a person fill out immigration or citizenship documents EXCEPT for the date and signature. (Notary Handbook)

NO. A notary is prohibited from advising people on immigration forms. (Notary Handbook)

TRUE. A notary public WHO IS ALSO a California registered immigration consultant CAN write on immigration forms the answers given to him by the client. (California Business and Professions Code 22441(a)(1); CGC 8223)

The amount that can be charged each person for completing a set of immigration papers is **$15.** (California Government Code 8223).

TRUE. A notary **is prohibited** from advertising that he is a notary if he also holds himself out to be an immigration consultant or specialist. (CGC 8223)

QUESTIONS

(Two credible witnesses)
The two credible witnesses must affirm (or swear) that they personally know the person who is the _____.

(Two credible witnesses)
T/F? The two credible witnesses must affirm (or swear) that it would be impossible (or very difficult) for the signer to obtain ID.

(Two credible witnesses)
The two credible witnesses must affirm (or swear) that the signer (does? / does not) have the ID to establish his own identity.

(Two credible witnesses)
T/F? The two credible witnesses must affirm (or swear) that the credible witnesses are not named in the document and don't have a financial interest.

Notary public journal entries must be recorded in _____ order.

A notary who willfully (intentionally) doesn't maintain his journal is guilty of a _____ offense. (CGC 8206(a) and 8228.1)

ANSWERS

(Two credible witnesses)
The two credible witnesses must affirm (or swear) that they personally know the person who is the **signer.** (California Civil Code 1185(b)(2))

(Two credible witnesses)
TRUE. The two credible witnesses must affirm (or swear) that it would be impossible (or very difficult) for the signer to obtain ID. (California Civil Code 1185(b)(2))

(Two credible witnesses)
The two credible witnesses must affirm (or swear) that the signer **DOESN'T** have the ID to establish his own identity. (California Civil Code 1185(b)(2))

(Two credible witnesses)
TRUE. The two credible witnesses must affirm or swear that the credible witnesses are not named in the document and don't have a financial interest. (California Civil Code 1185(b)(2))

Notary public journal entries must be recorded in **sequential** order. (CGC 8206(a)(1))

A notary who willfully (intentionally) doesn't maintain his journal is guilty of a **misdemeanor** offense. (CGC 8206(a) and 8228.1)

QUESTIONS

An immigration consultant who advertises that he is also a
_____ is a reason for refusal to appoint or to
punish a notary public.

Reasons for refusal to appoint or punish a notary public
includes failure to satisfy (pay) any court ordered
_____.

Reasons for refusal to appoint or punish a notary public
include failure to report the damage, theft, or loss of the
_____ journal.

Reasons for refusal to appoint or punish a notary public
includes translating "notary public" into the _____
language as "notario public".

Reasons for refusal to appoint or punish a notary public
includes willful _____ relating to a deed of trust.

Reasons for refusal to appoint or punish a notary public
includes filing a forged or false document that places an
_____ on a one family residence.

ANSWERS

An immigration consultant who advertises that he is also a **notary public** is a reason for refusal to appoint or to punish a notary public. (CGC 8223)

Reasons for refusal to appoint or punish a notary public includes failure to satisfy (pay) any court ordered **judgment**. (CGC 8214)

Reasons for refusal to appoint or punish a notary public include failure to report the damage, theft, or loss of the **SEQUENTIAL** journal. (CGC 8206, CGC 8207, and CGC 8206(b))

Reasons for refusal to appoint/punish a notary public includes translating "notary public" into the **Spanish** language as "notario public". (CGC 8219.5)

Reasons for refusal to appoint or punish a notary public includes willful **fraud** relating to a deed of trust. (CGC 8214)

Reasons for refusal to appoint or punish a notary public includes filing a forged or false document that places an **encumbrance** on a one family residence. (California Penal Code 115)

QUESTIONS

The date and _____ of all notary acts must be recorded in the notary journal.

The type of notarial act (may? / must?) be recorded in the journal.

The following can request a photocopy of a journal entry: 1) Secretary of State; 2) a member of the public; 3) _____

The notary must record in his journal the _____ of every instrument he notarizes.

T/F? The notary must record in his journal the signature of each person whose signature he notarizes.

The notary must indicate in his journal that the identity of the person was verified using _____ evidence.

ANSWERS

The date and **time** of all notary acts must be recorded in the notary journal. (CGC 8206(a)(2)(A))

The type of notarial act **MUST** be recorded in the journal. (Example: jurat, acknowledgment, etc.) (CGC 8206(a)(2)(A))

The following can request a photocopy copy of a journal entry: 1) Secretary of State; 2) a member of the public; **3) a peace officer investigating a crime**. (CGC 8206(a)(2)(A))

The notary must record in his journal the **character** of every instrument he notarizes. (CGC 8206(a)(2)(B))

TRUE. The notary must record in his journal the signature of each person whose signature he notarizes. (CGC 8206(a)(2)(C))

The notary must indicate in his journal that the identity of the person was verified using "**satisfactory** evidence". (CGC 8206(a)(2)(E))

QUESTIONS

The notary must record in his journal the type of ID used, the governmental agency that issued it, the date of issuance or _____, and the identification number of the ID.

If there is an oath or affirmation of two credible witnesses, the entry in the journal must contain the _____ of the credible witnesses and details of ID used by the credible witnesses.

If the notary doesn't charge a fee for the act, what notation should he make in the journal?

The right thumbprint of the individual signing the document is required (as part of the journal entry) when the notarized document is a power of attorney or any document affecting _____ property.

The right thumbprint (is? / is not?) required for a deed of reconveyance or for a nonjudicial foreclosure.

A(n) _____ is a declaration that is made before an official (example: a notary public) that under the person's free act and deed he did execute the instrument.

ANSWERS

The notary must record in his journal the type of ID used, the governmental agency that issued it, the date of issuance or **expiration**, and the identification number of the ID. (CGC 8206(a)(2)(D))

If there is an oath or affirmation of two credible witnesseses, the entry in the journal must contain the **signatures** of the credible witnesses and details of ID used by the credible witnesses. (CGC 8206(a)(2)(E))

If the notary doesn't charge a fee for the act, the notary should make the notation **"0"** in the "fee charged" space. (CGC 8206(a)(2)(F))

The right thumbprint of the individual signing the document is required (as part of the journal entry) when the notarized document is a power of attorney or any document affecting **real** property. (CGC 8206(a)(2)(G))

The right thumbprint **is not required** for a deed of reconveyance or for a nonjudicial foreclosure. (CGC 8206(a)(2)(G))

An **acknowledgment** is a declaration that is made before an official (example: a notary public) that under the person's free act and deed he did execute the instrument. (Legal Terms)

QUESTIONS

(For an acknowledgment)
If there are two credible witnesses, the witnesses must: 1) each sign the journal, and 2) the notary must record the details of the ID of the two _____.

Generally, the right _____ of the signer is required if the acknowledgment is for a document effecting real property (except trustee's deeds resulting from a decree of foreclosure or a nonjudicial foreclosure or a deed of reconveyance).

When must a Certificate of Acknowledgment be completed?

A Certificate of Acknowledgment verifies what?

Before a notary seal can be attached to a document, the certificate of acknowledgment must have the proper notarial _____.

The "_____ statement" is part of the Certificate of Acknowledgment. It states the county where the acknowledgment is being made.

ANSWERS

(For an acknowledgment)
If there are two credible witnesses, the witnesses must: 1) each sign the journal, and 2) the notary must record the details of the ID of the two **credible witnesses.** (CGC 8206(a)(2)(D) and (E))

Generally, the right **thumbprint** of the signer is required if the acknowledgment is for a document effecting real property (except trustee's deeds resulting from a decree of foreclosure or a nonjudicial foreclosure or a deed of reconveyance). CGC 8206)

A Certificate of Acknowledgment must be completed at the time when the notary signs the document and affixes the seal to the document. (California Civil Code 1188 and 1193)

The identity of the individual signing the document. (California Civil Code 1189)

Before a notary seal can be attached to a document, the certificate of acknowledgment must have the proper notarial **wording**. (California Civil Code 1188 and 1189)

The "**Venue** statement" is part of the Certificate of Acknowledgment. It states the county where the acknowledgment is being made. (Notary Handbook)

QUESTIONS

T/F? A notary who advertises in a language other than English must include that he is not an attorney and cannot give legal advice on immigration matters. He must also include the statutory fees that he charges.

Can a notary translate the words "notary public," as "notario publico" or "notario" (into Spanish)?

If a notary translates "notary public," as "notario publico" or "notario," into Spanish, his notary public commission may be suspended for not less than _____ year(s), or his commission may be revoked. A second offense may result in the permanent revocation of his commission.

Can a notary take an oral deposition by:
1) writing it longhand, or
2) typing it on an electronic device?

Generally, a deposition is providing oral or written testimony under oath, but _____ of a court proceeding.

A notary **MUST NOT** issue a confidential marriage license unless _____.

ANSWERS

TRUE. A notary who advertises in a language other than English must include that he is not an attorney and cannot give legal advice on immigration matters. He must also include the statutory fees that he charges. (CGC 8223)

NO. A notary public CANNOT translate the words "notary public," as "notario publico" or "notario" into Spanish. (CGC 8219.5.)

If a notary translates "notary public," as "notario publico" or "notario," into Spanish, his notary public commission may be suspended for not less than **ONE** year, or his commission may be revoked. A second offense may result in the permanent revocation of his commission. (CGC 8219.5)

YES. A notary may take an oral deposition by:
1) writing it longhand, or
2) typing it on an electronic device. (Civil Code 14)

Generally, a deposition is providing oral or written testimony under oath, but **outside** of a court proceeding. (Civil Code 14)

A notary **MUST NOT** issue a confidential marriage license **UNLESS he is approved by the county clerk.** (Notary Handbook)

QUESTIONS

MAXIMUM ALLOWABLE FEES
Certifying a copy of a power of attorney under California Probate Code 4307, $___.

MAXIMUM ALLOWABLE FEES
$.___ for notarizing veteran's application for a pension.

Can notaries appointed to military reservations charge a fee for notarial services? (CGC 8203.6)

A notary acting for the State, city, or county or public body cannot charge for notarizing an affidavit, application, or voucher for securing a _____.

Misconduct in connection with notarial acts may be punished by criminal, civil or _____ laws and proceedings.

Criminal misconduct may be a felony, misdemeanor or _____, depending on the conduct.

ANSWERS

MAXIMUM ALLOWABLE FEES
Certifying a copy of a power of attorney under California Probate Code 4307, **$15**. (CGC 8211)

NO fee may be charged for notarizing veteran's application for a pension. (CGC 8211)

NO. Notaries appointed to military reservations CANNOT charge a fee for any notarial services. (CGC 8203.6)

A notary acting for the State, city, or county or public body cannot charge for notarizing an affidavit, application, or voucher for securing a **PENSION** or **VETERAN'S BENEFITS** or **NOMINATION DOCUMENT**. (CGC 6106) (CGC 6107 & 8211(i)) (California Elections Code sec. 8080)

Misconduct in connection with notarial acts may be punished by criminal, civil or **ADMINISTRATIVE** laws and proceedings. (CGC 8214)

Criminal misconduct may be a felony, misdemeanor, or **INFRACTION,** depending on the conduct. (CGC 8214)

QUESTIONS

A <u>felony</u> is punishable by imprisonment in state prison or county jail. A _____ may also be imposed in addition to any imprisonment.

A misdemeanor is punishable by a term in jail, probation, a fine or _____.

An infraction is punishable by a_____.

If a person is guilty of civil misconduct, his commission may be revoked or suspended. If he is applying for a commission, his commission may be _____.

If a notary has a financial interest, can he perform a notarial act in connection with that transaction?

A notary public is prohibited from practicing law unless he is also a licensed _____.

ANSWERS

A felony is punishable by imprisonment in state prison or county jail. A **fine** may also be imposed in addition to any imprisonment. (Penal Code 17)

A misdemeanor is punishable by a term in jail, probation, a fine or **ALL THREE**. (Penal Code 17)

An infraction is punishable by a **FINE**. (Penal Code 17)

If a person is guilty of civil misconduct, his commission may be revoked or suspended. If he is applying for a commission, his commission may be **denied**. (California Government Code 8214.1(E))

NO. If a notary has a financial interest, he **CANNOT** perform a notarial act in connection with that transaction. (CGC 8224)

A notary public is prohibited from practicing law, unless he is also a licensed **CALIFORNIA ATTORNEY**. (CGC 8214.1(g); California Business and Professions Code 6215))

QUESTIONS

Civil Penalty: up to and including $750 or $1,500?
Willfully failing to discharge the duties or responsibilities
required of a notary public.

Civil Penalty: up to and including $750 or $1,500?
Failure to report to the Secretary of State that a seal is
destroyed, damaged, lost or stolen.

The penalty for failure to obtain a required thumbprint may
be the denial of an application, revocation, or suspension
of the notary commission. Also, the civil penalty is: up to
and including $_____.

The possible penalty for failure to obtain the satisfactory
evidence required of a credible witness is up to and
including $_____.

The possible penalty for willfully stating as true a material
fact that the notary knows to be false in a certificate of
acknowledgment is up to and including: $_____.

A notary who performs a fraudulent act in relation to a
deed of trust on real property (single-family residence with
not more than four dwelling units), is guilty of a
_____.

ANSWERS

Civil Penalty: up to and including $750 or $1,500?
Willfully failing to discharge the duties or responsibilities
required of a notary public: up to and including **$1,500**.
(CGC 8214.15)

Civil Penalty: up to and including $750 or $1,500?
Failure to report to the Secretary of State that a seal is
destroyed, damaged, lost or stolen: up to and including
$1.500. (CGC 8214.15)

The penalty for failure to obtain a required thumbprint may
be the denial of an application, revocation, or suspension
of the notary commission. Also, the civil penalty is: up to
and including **$2,500**. (CGC 8214.23)

The possible penalty for failure to obtain the satisfactory
evidence required of a credible witness is up to and
including **$10,000.** (California Civil Code 1185(b)(1)(B))

The possible penalty for willfully stating as true a material
fact that the notary knows to be false in a certificate of
acknowledgment is up to and including: **$10,000.**
(California Civil Code 1189(a)(2))

A notary who performs a fraudulent act in relation to a
deed of trust on real property (single-family residence with
not more than four dwelling units), is guilty of a **FELONY**.
(CGC 8214.2)

QUESTIONS

A person who is not a notary or a notary who performs unauthorized acts (single-family residence with not more than four dwelling units), is guilty of a _____.

A person who is not a notary but holds himself out to be a notary is guilty of a _____.

For filing a forged document with the county recorder (single-family residence with not more than four dwelling units) the penalty may include a fine not exceeding $_____.

A person making a false statement to a notary regarding single-family residence with not more than four dwelling units is guilty of a _____.

A person who forges a seal or handwriting is guilty of _____, punishable by imprisonment.

A person under oath who willfully states as true any material matter which he knows to be false, is guilty of _____.

ANSWERS

A person who is not a notary or a notary who performs unauthorized acts (single-family residence with not more than four dwelling units), is guilty is guilty of a **FELONY.** (CGC 8227.3)

A person who is not a notary but holds himself out to be a notary is guilty of a **misdemeanor**. (CGC 8227.1)

For filing a forged document with the county recorder (single-family residence with not more than four dwelling units) the penalty may include a fine not exceeding **$75,000**. (Penal Code 115.5)

A person making a false statement to a notary regarding single-family residence with not more than four dwelling units is guilty of a **felony**. (California Penal Code 115.5(b))

A person who forges a seal or handwriting is guilty of **forgery**, punishable by imprisonment. (California Penal Code 473)

A person under oath who willfully states as true any material matter which he knows to be false, is guilty of **PERJURY**. (California Penal Code 118)

QUESTIONS

A person who willfully (intentionally) fails to perform a duty relating to the official journal or to control the notarial seal is guilty of a _____.

A notary who makes or delivers a false certificate is guilty of a _____.

A person who practices law but is not a member of the bar is guilty of a _____.

Failure to notify the Secretary of State of a change of principal place of business or residence address is punishable as a(n) _____ (fine not to exceed $500). (CGC 8213.5)

Failure to notify the Secretary of State of a name change is punishable as an infraction (fine not to exceed $____).

T/F? There are several exceptions to the requirement that the oath and bond of a notary must be filed within 30 days of the start of the commission.

ANSWERS

A person who willfully (intentionally) fails to perform a duty relating to the official journal or to control the notarial seal is guilty of a **misdemeanor**. (CGC 8228.1)

A notary who makes or delivers a false certificate is guilty of a **misdemeanor**. (CGC 6203.)

A person who practices law but is not a member of the bar is guilty of a **misdemeanor**. (California Business and Professions Code 6126)

Failure to notify the Secretary of State of a change of principal place of business or residence address is punishable as an **infraction** (fine not to exceed $500). (CGC 8213.5)

Failure to notify the Secretary of State of a name change is punishable as an infraction (fine not to exceed **$500)**. (CGC 8213.6)

FALSE. There are no exceptions. (CGC 8213)

QUESTIONS

Reasons for refusal to appoint or punish a notary public includes illegally practicing the profession of _____.

T/F? Reasons for refusal to appoint or punish a notary public includes charging the statutory fee.

T/F? Reasons for refusal to appoint or punish a notary public include fraud, dishonesty, or deceit.

T/F? Reasons for refusal to appoint or punish a notary includes failure to complete the acknowledgment form when the notary signs and fixes the seal on the document.

T/F? Reasons for refusal to appoint or punish a notary public includes failure to administer the required affirmation or oath.

T/F? Reasons for refusal to appoint or punish a notary public includes executing a false certificate.

ANSWERS

Reasons for refusal to appoint or punish a notary public includes illegally practicing the profession of **LAW**. (California Business and Professions Code 6125)

FALSE. Reasons for refusal to appoint or punish a notary public includes charging **MORE THAN** the statutory fee. (CGC 8214)

TRUE. Reasons for refusal to appoint or punish a notary public include fraud, dishonesty, or deceit. (CGC 8214)

TRUE. Reason for refusal to appoint or punish a notary includes failure to complete the acknowledgment form when the notary signs and fixes the seal on the document. (CGC 8214)

TRUE. Reasons for refusal to appoint or punish a notary public includes failure to administer the required affirmation or oath. (CGC 8214)

TRUE. Reasons for refusal to appoint or punish a notary public includes executing a false certificate. (CGC 8214)

QUESTIONS

Civil Penalty: up to and including $750 or $1,500?
Failing to complete the acknowledgment at the time the notary public's signature and seal are attached to the document.

Civil Penalty: up to and including $750 or $1,500?
Failing to administer the oath or affirmation.

Civil Penalty: up to and including $750 or $1,500?
Execution a certificate which contains a statement that the notary knows is false.

Civil Penalty: up to and including $750 or $1,500?
Failing to provide information to the Secretary of State within 30 days of a written request by the Secretary of State.

Civil Penalty: up to and including $750 or $1,500?
A notary who advertises or holds himself out to be an immigration consultant or specialist.

Civil Penalty: up to and including $750 or $1,500?
Improperly advertising notarial services in a language other than English or translating the words "notary public" into Spanish.

ANSWERS

Civil Penalty: up to and including $750 or $1,500?
Failing to complete the acknowledgment at the time the
notary public's signature and seal are attached to the
document: up to and including **$750.** (CGC 8214.15)

Civil Penalty: up to and including $750 or $1,500?
Failing to administer the oath or affirmation: up to and
including **$750.** (CGC 8214.15)

Civil Penalty: up to and including $750 or $1,500?
Execution a certificate which contains a statement that the
notary knows is false: up to and including **$1,500.** (CGC
8207.4)

Civil Penalty: up to and including $750 or $1,500?
Failing to provide information to the Secretary of State
within 30 days of a written request by the Secretary of
State: up to and including **$750.** (CGC 8214.15)

Civil Penalty: up to and including $750 or $1,500?
A notary who advertises or holds himself out to be an
immigration consultant or specialist: up to and including
$1,500. (CGC 8214.15)

Civil Penalty: up to and including $750 or $1,500?
Improperly advertising notarial services in a language other
than English or translating the (CGC 8214.15) words
"notary public" into Spanish: up to and including **$1,500**.

MULTIPLE CHOICE QUESTIONS

The following pages help you to reinforce your understanding by providing multiple choice questions:

After you master the multiple-choice questions, continue to the 5 practice exams.

PLEASE NOTE

Whenever you answer a question incorrectly, review that section of law.

Also, make sure you are comfortable with all the legal terms. They will help you to understand and become comfortable with the law, both for the exam and later during your notary public career.

———————

QUESTIONS

What is the title of the California official who appoints notaries and prescribes the written examination that applicants must pass?

A. Governor
B. Attorney General
C. Secretary of State
D. State Controller

The geographical jurisdiction of a notary (the geographical area where a notary can act in his official capacity) is:
A. only the county where the notary oath and bond are filed.
B. only the county where the notary oath and bond are filed and the surrounding counties.
C. only the county of residence of the notary public.
D. all the counties in the State of California.

John Tannor, a notary public who lives and works in Calaveras County, California, is visiting a friend in Clark county, Nevada. His friend asks that he notarize her signature on a document. Based on the preceding facts, John Tannor:
A. must notarize the signature.
B. must charge a fee of $20.
C. may notarize the document because he knows the identity of his friend.
D. none of the above

Everyone who wishes to apply for appointment as a California notary public must be at least ___ years of age.
A. 35
B. 24
C. 21
D. 18

ANSWERS

C. Secretary of State (CGC 8200)

D. all the counties in the State of California. (CGC 8200)

D. none of the above (The geographical jurisdiction of a notary (the geographical area where a notary can act) is limited to all the counties in the State of California.) (CGC 8200)

D. 18 (CGC sections 8201)

QUESTIONS

Generally, a person who wants to be appointed as a California notary must be a California resident at the time of appointment. One exception to this is a person who:
A. is a war veteran.
B. is over the age of 65.
C. is appointed to serve on a military or naval reservation.
D. None of the above are correct.

A person applying for a notary commission must complete satisfactorily a course approved by the Secretary of State of California. The course is ___ hours long.
A. 3   C. 9
B. 6   D. 12

An applicant may complete a ____hour refresher course if he meets the following two conditions: (1) he currently holds an active notary public commission AND (2) he has already completed a 6-hour course as part of a previous application.
A. 2   C. 4
B. 3   D. 5

In addition to passing the notary public written examination, an applicant must submit his fingerprints within ____ to be used in his background check.
A. 30 days   C. 6 months
B. 3 months   D. one year

ANSWERS

C. is appointed to serve on a military or naval reservation. (CGC 8201(a)(1) and 8203.1)

B. 6 (CGC section 8201(a)(3))

B. 3 hour (CGC 8201(b)(2))

D. one year (CGC 8201.1(a))

QUESTIONS

The penalty for violating regulations regarding approved vendors may be an amount up to and including _____ for each violation.
A. $750
B. $1,000
C. $1,500
D. $7,500

When a notary executes a jurat, the affiant must:
A. pay a fee of $25.
B. sign the document in front of the notary.
C. be accompanied by three witnesses.
D. none of the above

What is the title of the certificate where a person swears (or affirms) that the contents of the document are true and correct?
A. acknowledgment
B. deposition
C. jurat
D. none of the above

A person must appear before a notary for the following:
  1. an acknowledgment
  2. a jurat
A. 1 only
B. 2 only
C. both 1 and 2
D. neither 1 nor 2

ANSWERS

B. $1,000 (CGC 8201.2)

B. sign the document in front of the notary. (CGC 8202)

C. jurat (CGC 8202)

B. 2 only (for a jurat) (Civil Code 1189 and CGC 8202)

QUESTIONS

Which of the following two statements are correct? A notary public can complete a jurat:

1. that was mailed to him, but where the person did not appear before the notary.
2. that was mailed to him by a person the notary knows personally, even though the person did not appear before the notary.

A. Number 1 only is correct.   C. Numbers 1 and 2 are incorrect.
B. Number 2 only is correct.   D. Numbers 1 and 2 are correct.

Which of the following statements is not correct? In a jurat the notary public certifies the following:

A. the identity of the signer based on "satisfactory evidence."
B. the signer signed in the presence of the notary.
C. an affirmation or oath was administered by a witness.
D. the identity of the signer.

A notarial certificate:

A. must be in a foreign language that is the same as the language of the document.
B. may be in English or a foreign language.
C. must be in English.
D. must be in the language preferred by the person signing the document.

To be acceptable ID, a foreign passport must have been stamped by:

A. the California Secretary of State.
B. the FBI.
C. the U.S. Immigration or Naturalization Service or the U.S. Citizenship and Immigration Service.
D. none of the above

ANSWERS

C. Numbers 1 and 2 are incorrect. (The person MUST personally appear before the notary public.) (CGC 8202)

C. an affirmation or oath was administered by a witness. (This is NOT correct because it should read, "an affirmation or oath was administered by **the notary**.) (CGC 8202)

C. must be in English. (California Civil Code 1188, 1189 and 1195; CGC 8202)

C. the U.S. Immigration or Naturalization Service or the U.S. Citizenship and Immigration Service. (California Civil Code 1185(b)(4))

QUESTIONS

A private employer and a notary may agree that the notary during his employment:
A. charge greater than the maximum fee.
B. the notary may perform only notarial services for transactions directly connected to the business.
C. charge double the statutory fee.
D. none of the above.

Which one of the following statements is not correct? A person appointed to be a notary in a military reservation must:
A. be not less than 21 years of age.
B. be a United States citizen
C. perform notarial services on a military reservation located within California.
D. be a federal civil service employee at the military reservation.

A jurat executed on a military or naval reservation must contain the name of the State and the _____ where the jurat is executed.
A. name of the county
B. name of the city
C. name of the reservation
D. none of the above

A notary public appointed for a military reservation must charge:
A. the minimum fees.
B. the maximum fees.
C. no fees.
D. none of the above.

ANSWERS

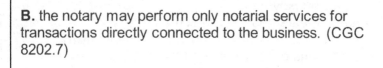

B. the notary may perform only notarial services for transactions directly connected to the business. (CGC 8202.7)

A. be not less than 21 years of age. (This is not correct. The correct age is 18.) (CGC 8203.1)

C. name of the reservation (CGC 8203.5)

C. no fees. (CGC 8203.6)

QUESTIONS

The term of office of a notary public is:
A. 3 years (if the notary qualified with a 3-hour course).
B. 6 years.
C. 2 years.
D. 4 years.

If a check by a notary public applicant in payment for the commission, application, examination, and fingerprint report is not accepted by the bank, Secretary of State may:
A. fine the applicant $100.
B. reduce the applicant's score on the notary public written examination by 10 points.
C. cancel the commission.
D. none of the above

Choose the best answer: A notary public employed by a financial institution is empowered during his employment to:
A. demand acceptance and payment of foreign and inland bills of exchange.
B. charge double the maximum notarial fees.
C. Neither A nor B.
D. Both A and B.

A notary public:
A. can notarize all incomplete documents.
B. is prohibited from notarizing incomplete documents.
C. can notarize an incomplete document if it will be completed later in his presence.
D. none of the above

ANSWERS

D. 4 years. (CGC 8204) (Required class and exam must be retaken every four years before the expiration of the term.)

C. cancel the commission. (CGC 8204.1)

A. demand acceptance and payment of foreign and inland bills of exchange. (CGC 8205)

B. is prohibited from notarizing incomplete documents. (CGC 8205)

QUESTIONS

Grounds for denial, revocation, or suspension of appointment and commission include all the following, except:
A. charging more than the statutory fee.
B. conviction of a felony.
C. failure to submit to the Secretary of State requested documents.
D. securing the official journal and seal.

An agreement between a notary and a private employer may state that the following may be required to be turned over to the employer:
A. the notary journal
B. notary fees collected
C. the notary seal
D. the notary public seal and journal

How many days does a notary have to answer a written request for information from the California Secretary of State?
A. 10 days
B. 15 days
C. 20 days
D. 30 days

Which of the following is authorized to have access to the notary journal without the notary being present?
A. an employee of the notary
B. the employer of the notary
C. a trusted and mature family member
D. no one

ANSWERS

D. securing the official journal and seal. (This should read, "FAILURE to secure the official journal and seal.) (CGC 8205, 8214.1, 8219.5, and 8223)

B. notary fees collected (CGC 8205(b)(2))

D. 30 days (CGC 8205(b)(2))

D. no one (CGC 8206(a)(1))

QUESTIONS

The notary public journal must be surrendered:
A. to any employer, even if the notary has not worked for that employer.
B. to the county vital statistics office and the county real estate tax office.
C. to a peace officer investigating a crime who has reasonable cause to believe the journal contains evidence of the criminal offense.
D. none of the above.

If a police officer seizes a notary public journal, the notary shall notify the Secretary of State by certified mail within _____.
A. 5 days
B. 10 days
C. 15 days
D. 30 days

What is the title of the subpoena that may be served on a notary to provide his journal for copying?
A. information subpoena
B. lis pendens
C. subpoena duces tecum
D. none of the above

If the document being notarized is a deed of trust, quitclaim dee, or a deed, the person signing the document must (unless exempted by law) _____.
A. pay double the statutory fee.
B. place his thumbprint in the journal.
C. provide three witnesses.
D. be over the age of 40.

ANSWERS

C. to a peace officer investigating a crime who has reasonable cause to believe the journal contains evidence of the criminal offense. (CGC 8206 (d))

B. 10 days (CGC 8206 (d))

C. subpoena duces tecum (CGC 8206 (d))

B. place his thumbprint in the journal. (CGC 8206 (G))

QUESTIONS

If there are 1 or 2 credible witnesses used to establish identity, which of the credible witnesses must sign the notary journal?
A. There is a requirement for signature only if there is one credible witness.
B. There is a requirement for signatures only if there are two credible witnesses.
C. In both cases there is no requirement for signatures.
D. The credible witnesses must sign the journal whether there are one or two credible witnesses.

Which of the following two statements are correct? A notary public can complete an acknowledgment:
1. that was mailed to him, but where the person did not appear before the notary.
2. that was mailed to him by a person the notary knows personally, even though the person did not appear before the notary.
A. 1 only is correct.   C. 1 and 2 are both incorrect.
B. 2 only is correct.   D. 1 and 2 are both correct.

Which one of the following statements is not correct?
A proof of execution by a subscribing witness cannot be used in instance where:
A. the document is a quitclaim deed.
B. the document is a power of attorney.
C. the document is a mortgage.
D. where a thumbprint is not required.

Which of the following is not correct?
The notary journal must contain:
A. the date, time, and type of each notarial act.
B. the character of every instrument that is acknowledged.
C. the signature of each person whose signature is being notarized.
D. the signatures of all persons who witness the making of a mark that is being notarized.

ANSWERS

D. The credible witnesses must sign the journal whether there are one or two credible witnesses. (CGC 8206(a)(E)

C. Numbers 1 and 2 are both incorrect. (Unless there are credible witnesses, the person MUST personally appear before the notary public.) (CGC 8206)

D. where a thumbprint is not required. (This statement is not correct. It should read, "where a thumbprint IS required.) (CGC 27287 and Civil Code 1195(b)(1) and (2))

D. the signatures of all persons who witness the making of a mark that is being notarized. (This is not a requirement of CGC 8206. Also, in the law relating to making of a mark in front of a notary, the signatures of the witnesses are specifically stated as NOT required.)

QUESTIONS

Which of the following ID information is not required to be recorded in the notary journal?
A. the type of identifying document (Example: passport)
B. the serial or other identifying number of the ID document
C. the date of issue or the date of expiration of the ID document
D. the physical condition of the ID document

Which of the following statements regarding a single credible witness is not correct? The single credible witness must sign the notary journal, or the notary must indicate in the journal all the following:
A. the type of ID presented by the credible witness
B. the identification number of the ID document
C. the issuance date or expiration date of the ID document
D. the home address of the credible witness

Which of the following statements regarding a notary public journal is not correct?
A. The notary must keep one or more active journals at a time.
B. The notary must record in the journal all notarial acts performed.
C. The acts recorded in the journal must be in sequential order.
D. The journal must be kept in a secure area. It must also be under the exclusive control of the notary.

Which one of the following four choices lists an item that is not required to be included in a notary public journal?
A. Date and time of every official notarial act
B. The type of each official act (Example: jurat)
C. The signature and address of the person(s) whose signature is being notarized.
D. A statement that "satisfactory evidence" was used to identify the person taking the oath (or making an acknowledgment).

ANSWERS

D. the <u>physical condition</u> of the ID document This is not correct because it is not one of the requirements listed in CGC 8206(a)(2)(D))

D. the home address of the credible witness (This is not correct because it is not a requirement of the law. (CGC 8206(a)(2)(D)).
The requirements (A, B, and C) also apply when there are two credible witnesses. (CGC 8206(a)(2)(E))

A. The notary must keep one or more active journals at a time. (This is NOT correct because ONLY ONE journal may be kept active at any one time. (CGC 8206(a))

C. The signature and address of the person(s) whose signature is being notarized. (This statement is NOT correct because the address of the person is NOT required to be recorded in the notary public journal.) (CGC 8206(a))

QUESTIONS

Which of the following two statements (1 and 2) are correct?
1. The fee charged for the notarial service must be recorded in the journal.
2. The right thumbprint of the person signing the document being notarized must be recorded in the journal in all cases.
A. Only 1 is correct.
B. Only 2 is correct.
C. Both 1 and 2 are not correct.
D. Both 1 and 2 are not correct.

Which of the following four choices is not correct? If a notary public journal is damaged or rendered unusable, etc. the notary must inform the Secretary of State by certified or registered mail and include the following information:
A. the notary public commission number
B. the commission expiration date
C. a copy of the police report
D. the time periods of the journal entries

Which of the following is not correct? The notary public must inform the Secretary of State of the loss, destruction, etc. of the notary journal and must include the following information:
A. the notary public commission number
B. a photocopy of the police report (if applicable)
C. the notary public commencement date
D. the time periods of the journal entries recorded in the journal

---

If a member of the public requests in writing a copy of a transaction recorded in the journal, the notary must respond within ___ business days and may charge thirty cents ($.30) per copy page.
A. 10
B. 15
C. 20
D. 30

ANSWERS

A. Only 1 is correct. (Statement 2 is not correct because the right thumbprint is only required (unless it is a physical impossibility) when the document being notarized is for certain specified documents relating to real property). Also, if there is no right thumb, the left thumb or any finger may be used, or if no thumb or finger is available, the notary can indicate that in the journal. (CGC 8206(a))

C. a copy of the police report (This is NOT correct because a copy of the police report must be included WHEN APPLICABLE, usually when an offense has been committed, and not when it is damaged due to negligence.) (CGC 8206(b))

C. the notary public commencement date This is not correct. It should read, the notary public <u>expiration</u> date." (CGC 8206(b))

B. 15 business days (CGC 8206(c) and 8206.5) Note that it is 15 <u>BUSINESS</u> days (and NOT 15 <u>calendar</u> days.)

QUESTIONS

How many days does a notary public have to respond to a written request from a person for a photocopy of a line item in his journal?
A. 10 business days
B. 10 calendar days
C. 15 business days
D. 15 calendar days

A written request to a notary by a person must include the following information:
A. the names of the parties
B. the type of document
C. month and year of notarization
D. all the above

How much can a notary public charge a member of the public for each photocopy prepared in response to a request by a member of the public?
A. 10 cents
B. 15 cents
C. 30 cents
D. 45 cents

Which of the following four choices is not correct? A notary must surrender his journal:
A. when required by law.
B. to a peace officer who believes the journal has evidence of a criminal offense.
C. upon request of the county clerk where the notary commission is filed.
D. to his employer if the employer requests the journal.

ANSWERS

C. 15 business days (Even if no such journal entry exists, the notary public must still respond within 15 business days.) (CGC 8206 (c))

D. all the above (CGC 8206(c) (The notary must respond within 15 business days and may charge thirty cents ($.30) per copy page.)

C. 30 cents per photocopy page (CGC 8206(c) and 8206.5)

D. to his employer if the employer requests the journal. (The notary is prohibited from surrendering his journal to his employer.) (CGC 8206(d))

QUESTIONS

When a notary surrenders his journal to a peace officer, he must obtain a receipt. The notary is also required to notify the Secretary of State within _____ by certified mail.
A. 5 days
B. 10 days
C. 15 days
D. 20 days

If a notary public commission is no longer valid, the seal:
A. must be stored in a secure place.
B. may only be used for 30 more days.
C. must be destroyed.
D. none of the above.

If the notary needs a new stamp, he:
A. just asks the vendor for a replacement stamp.
B. must take the 6-hour class.
C. must obtain a certificate of authorization from the Secretary of State.
D. none of the above.

Which of the following statements regarding a notary public seal is not correct?
A. The seal must be photographically reproducible.
B. In addition to the notary rubber stamp, a notary may not use an embosser seal.
C. The seal must contain the words "Notary Public."
D. The seal must contain the name of the notary public (which must be the same as on the notary public commission).

ANSWERS

B. 10 days (CGC 8206(d))

C. must be destroyed. (CGC 8207)

C. must obtain a certificate of authorization from the Secretary of State. (CGC 8207.3(e))

B. In addition to the rubber stamp, a notary may not use an embosser seal.
This statement is not correct because the notary **MAY** use an embosser seal in addition to the rubber seal. (CGC 8207)

QUESTIONS

Which of the following statements regarding what a notary public seal must contain is not correct?
A. It must contain the name of the county where the oath of office and bond of the notary are filed.
B. It must contain the commencement date of the notary public's commission.
C. It must contain the commission number of the notary.
D. It must contain the ID number assigned to the seal manufacturer or vendor.

Which of the following statements regarding a notary public seal is not correct?
A. The seal may be circular (not over two inches).
B. The seal may be rectangular (not more than 1 inch in width by 2 and ½ inches in length).
C. The seal must have serrated edge (or milled edge border).
D. The seal cannot be a rubber stamp seal.

Documents that are acknowledged may be recorded by the county clerk. Because of this, the seal must be

_____.
A. 4 inches in diameter (if circular).
B. 3 and ½ by 4 inches (if rectangular).
C. used in conjunction with red ink.
D. legible.

A notary public seal shall not be duplicated, sold, manufactured, or offered for sale without the authorization by the _____.
A. county clerk
B. county court
C. Secretary of State
D. State Comptroller

ANSWERS

B. It must contain the commencement date of the notary public's commission. (This is not correct because the seal must contain the date of **EXPIRATION** of the notary public's commission.) (CGC 8207)

D. The seal cannot be a rubber stamp seal. (This statement is not correct because the seal **MAY** be a rubber stamp seal.) (CGC 8207)

D. legible. (CGC 8207)

C. Secretary of State (CGC 8207.2)

QUESTIONS

If the seal of a notary is misplaced, lost, broken, damaged, destroyed or becomes unusable, the notary must give written notice to the _____ who will (within 5 days) issue a certificate of authorization for the notary to acquire a new seal.
A. county clerk
B. State Professions Office
C. county court
D. Secretary of State

Which of the following statements is not correct?
A. A sequential journal shall not be surrendered to an employer when the notary ends his employment.
B. A notary public who intentionally (willfully) does not maintain his journal properly is guilty of a felony.
C. If the notary commission is no longer valid, the notary must deliver all notarial records and journal(s) to the clerk of county.
D. The records cited in "C" must be delivered within 30 days.

Which of the following four choices is not correct?
The notary or his representative must destroy or deface the seal at the time of the:
A. resignation of the notary.
B. termination of the notary commission.
C. revocation of the notary commission.
D. extended vacation of the notary.

If the employee notary (of a public employer) resigns or is terminated, this is considered:
A. the same as a renewal of the commission of the notary.
B. the same as a temporary suspension of the notary public commission.
C. the same as been found guilty of a misdemeanor.
D. the same as a resignation of the commission of the notary.

ANSWERS

D. Secretary of State (CGC 8207.3)

B. A notary public who intentionally (willfully) does not maintain his journal is guilty of a felony. (This is NOT correct because a notary public who intentionally (willfully) does not maintain his journal is guilty of a MISDEMEANOR.) (CGC 8209)

D. extended vacation of the notary. (This is not correct. It should read, "**death** of the notary." (CGC 8209 (b))

D. the same as a resignation of the commission of the notary. (CGC 8200)

QUESTIONS

The notarial fees listed in Government Code 8211 are:
A. minimum fees.
B. suggested fees.
C. maximum fees.
D. average fees.

The maximum fee for taking an acknowledgment or proof of a deed, or other instrument, to include the seal and the writing of the certificate is _____ for each signature taken.
A. $5
B. $10
C. $15
D. $20

The maximum fee for administering an oath or affirmation to one person and executing the jurat, including the seal is

_____.
A. $2
B. $5
C. $10
D. $15

The maximum fee for all services rendered in connection with the taking of any deposition: $_____, and in addition: $_____ for administering the oath to the witness, and $_____ for the certificate to the deposition.
A. $10 .... $10 .... $10
B. $20 .... $10 .... $10
C. $30 .... $7 ...... $7
D. none of the above

ANSWERS

C. maximum fees. (A notary may if he wishes, charge a smaller fee, or no fee at all.) (CGC 8211)

C. $15 (CGC 8211)

D. $15 (CGC 8211)

C. $30 .... $7 ...... $7 (CGC 8211)

QUESTIONS

The maximum fee per line item copied from the notary public's journal is _____.
A. 10 cents per copy page
B. 20 cents per copy page
C. 30 cents per copy page
D. none of the above

The maximum fee for certifying a copy of a power of attorney under Section 4307 of the Probate Code is

_____.
A. $2
B. $5
C. $15
D. No fee is permitted to be charged.

The maximum fee that may be charged to notarize signatures on vote by mail ballot identification envelopes or other voting materials is _____.
A. $2
B. $5
C. $10
D. No fee is permitted to be charged.

The maximum fee for an acknowledgment or proof of a deed (or other instrument, including the seal and writing the certificate) is _____ for each signature acknowledged.
A. $10
B. $15
C. $20
D. $30

ANSWERS

C. 30 cents per copy page (CGC 8211)

C. $15 (CGC 8211)

D. No fee is permitted to be charged. (CGC 8211)

B. $15 (CGC 8211)

QUESTIONS

The maximum fee that may be charged to a United States military veteran for notarization of an application or a claim for a pension, allotment, allowance, compensation, insurance, or any other veteran's benefit is _____.
A. $2
B. $5
C. $10
D. No fee is permitted to be charged.

The required notary public bond (which must be filed with the clerk of county) must be in the amount of:
A. $10,000   C. $20,000
B. $15,000   D. $30,000

After a notary public commission is issued, the person has ___ days to 1) file an oath of office with the clerk of county, and 2) file a surety bond with the office of the clerk of county.
A. 10 days   C. 30 days
B. 20 days   D. 60 days

A notary who submits an application for a name change to the Secretary of State must within _____ from the date that the amended commission is issued, file a new oath of office and an amendment to the bond with the county clerk in which the principal place of business is located.
A. 10 days   C. 20 days
B. 15 days   D. 30 days

ANSWERS

D. No fee is permitted to be charged. (CGC 8211)

B. $15,000 (CGC 8212) (The notary is personally liable for all damages. Also, if damages are due to negligence or misconduct, the notary may be required to reimburse the bond company.)

C. 30 days (CGC 8213)

D. 30 days (CGC 8213)

QUESTIONS

The fee to submit an address change form or address change letter is _____.
A. $10
B. $15
C. $20
D. none of the above

A change of address by the notary must be reported to _____ within 30 days by certified mail.
A. county clerk
B. Secretary of State.
C. the State Comptroller.
D. the county court.

The notary public applicant must state in his application the name of a business only if he plans to _____ of his notarial services for it.
A. perform fifty percent
B. perform a majority
C. perform all
D. perform a third

Willful failure to notify the Secretary of State of a change of address shall be punishable as an infraction by a fine of not more than _____.
A. $100
B. $500
C. $1,000
D. $1,500

ANSWERS

D. none of the above (NO fee is required.) (CGC 8213)

B. Secretary of State. (No fee is required for filing an address change.) (CGC 8213.5)

B. perform a majority (CGC 8201.5 and 8213.5)

B. $500 (CGC 8213.6)

QUESTIONS

Which of the following two statements are correct?
A person who applies for a notary public commission must disclose:
    1. all arrests for which a trial is pending.
    2. all convictions.
A. Only choice 1 is correct.
B. Only choice 2 is correct.
C. Both choices 1 and 2 are correct.
D. Neither choice 1 nor choice 2 is correct.

Grounds for refusal, revocation, or suspension of notary public commission do not include:
A. Substantial misstatement in notary application.
B. Conviction of an infraction.
C. Denial of a professional license due to dishonesty.
D. Failure to faithfully discharge duties of a notary public.

Grounds for refusal, revocation, or suspension of notary public commission do not include:
A. Adjudicated liable for damages due to fraud, misrepresentation, etc.
B. Misleading advertising regarding notarial powers.
C. The practice of law, where notary is not a California attorney.
D. Charging less than the statutory fees.

Grounds for refusal, revocation, or suspension of notary public commission do not include:
A. Commission of any act involving dishonesty.
B. Failure to complete an acknowledgment timely.
C. Failure to administer a required oath.
D. Unknowingly executing a false certificate.

ANSWERS

C. Both choices 1 and 2 are correct. (CGC 8214.1(a))

B. Conviction of an infraction. (This should read, "Conviction of a <u>felony</u>.") (CGC 8214.1(b))

D. Charging less than the statutory fees. (This should read, "Charging <u>more</u> than the statutory fees.") (CGC 8214.1(h))

D. Unknowingly executing a false certificate. (This should read, "<u>Knowingly</u> executing a false certificate.") (CGC 8214.1(l))

QUESTIONS

Grounds for refusal, revocation, or suspension of notary public commission do not include:
A. Securing the sequential journal.
B. Failure to pay a judgment as demanded by the Secretary of State.
C. Willful failure to provide access to the journal after a demand by a peace officer.
D. Charging more than the statutory fees.

Which of the following is not a correct maximum civil penalty for the stated offense committed by a notary?
A. dishonesty, fraud, deceit: $1,500
B. misleading advertising by a notary: $750
C. charging more than the maximum allowable fees: $750
D. failure to complete the acknowledgment at proper time: $1,500

Which of the following is not a correct maximum civil penalty for the stated offense committed by a notary?
A. failing to administer the oath or affirmation: $750.
B. executing a false certificate: $750
C. failing to respond to the Secretary of State within 30 days: $750
D. using the words "notario publico": $1,500

Which of the following is not a correct maximum civil penalty for the stated offense committed by a notary?
A. willful failure to discharge notary public responsibilities: $1,500
B. Failure to report to the Secretary of State a lost seal: $1,500
C. Failure to obtain required thumbprint: $1,500
D. Failure to obtain required satisfactory evidence: $10,000

ANSWERS

A. Securing the sequential journal. (This should read, "Not securing the sequential journal.") (CGC 8214.1 (o))

B. misleading advertising by a notary: $750 (The correct maximum civil penalty is $1,500.) (CGC 8214.15)

B. executing a false certificate: $750 (The correct maximum civil penalty is $1,500.) (CGC 8214.15)

C. Failure to obtain required thumbprint: $1,500 (The correct maximum civil penalty is $2,500.) (CGC 8214.15)

QUESTIONS

Performing a fraudulent notarial act relating to a deed of trust (real property not more than four dwelling units) is a:
A. infraction.
B. misdemeanor.
C. felony.
D. none of the above

The civil penalty for failure to provide access to a sequential journal when properly requested by a peace officer is an amount not exceeding $_____.
A. $500
B. $1,000
C. $1,500
D. $2,500

The civil penalty for failure to obtain a required thumbprint in a sequential journal is an amount not exceeding $_____.
A. $500
B. $1,000
C. $1,500
D. $2,500

If a person is convicted of any crime relating to misconduct on the part of the notary, the court must:
  1) revoke the notary commission, and
  2) order the notary to surrender the notary seal to the court.
A. 1 only is correct.   C. 1 and 2 are both correct.
B. 2 only is correct.   D. 1 and 2 are both incorrect.

ANSWERS

C. felony. (CGC 8214.2)

D. $2,500 (CGC 8214.21)

D. $2,500 (CGC 8214.23(a))

C. 1 and 2 are both correct. (CGC 8214.8)

QUESTIONS

When advertising in the Spanish language, can a notary translate "Notary Public" as "notario publico"?
A. Yes, if the periodical is published by a non-profit group.
B. No. He is prohibited from doing so.
C. Yes if the periodical is entirely in the Spanish language.
D. none of the above

A notary who translates "Notary Public" as "notario publico" in the Spanish language is subject to suspension of his notary public commission for one year (for the first offense) and for the second offense:
A. suspension of commission for two more years.
B. fine of $10,000.
C. revocation of commission.
D. none of the above

A person who intentionally destroys notary public records belonging to a notary is guilty of:
A. an infraction.
B. a misdemeanor.
C. a felony.
D. none of the above

A notary public cannot advertise that he is a notary public in addition to being a(n) _____ specialist.
A. income tax
B. immigration
C. EMT
D. none of the above

ANSWERS

B. No. He is prohibited from doing so. (CGC 8219.5)

C. revocation of commission. (CGC 8219.5)

B. a misdemeanor. (CGC 8221)

B. immigration (Government Code 8223)

QUESTIONS

A notary public who is a qualified and bonded immigration consultant may enter data provided by the client on immigration forms and may charge each client $_____ for each set of forms.
A. $15
B. $20
C. $30
D. $40

Generally, can a notary public notarize a document if he has a financial interest in the document?
A. Yes, in all cases.
B. Yes if he does not charge a notarial fee.
C. Yes if he is requested to do so.
D. None of the above.

A person who influences a notary to do an improper act is guilty of a(n) _____.
A. infraction
B. misdemeanor
C. felony
D. unethical conduct

A person who holds himself out to be a notary but is not a notary is guilty of _____.
A. an infraction
B. a misdemeanor
C. a felony
D. civil contempt

ANSWERS

A. $15 (CGC 8223)

D. None of the above. Generally, the notary cannot notarize documents in which he has a beneficial or financial interest. (CGC 8224)

B. misdemeanor (CGC 8225)

B. a misdemeanor (CGC 8227.1)

QUESTIONS

If a notary public intentionally (willfully) surrenders his seal to a person not authorized by law to have it, or if the notary fails to secure his journal, he is guilty of:
A. an infraction
B. a petty offense
C. a misdemeanor
D. a felony

If a notary intentionally does not properly maintain his notary journal, he is guilty of _____.
A. an infraction
B. a misdemeanor
C. a felony
D. none of the above

A notary can certify copies of the following vital records:
A. birth certificates.
B. marriage certificates.
C. death certificates.
D. none of the above

Generally, if a notary executes a jurat and the document contains the identity of the affiant and age (including the birthdate), the notary shall require verification of the birthdate or age by either:
1. A certified copy of the person's birth certificate, or
2. An identification card or driver's license issued by the Department of Motor Vehicles.

A. 1 only   C. Neither 1 nor 2
B. 2 only   D. Either 1 or 2

ANSWERS

C. a misdemeanor (CGC 8228.1) If a notary public intentionally (willfully) surrenders his seal to a person not authorized by law to have it, or the notary fails to secure his journal, he is guilty of a **misdemeanor.**

B. a misdemeanor (CGC 8228.1)

D. none of the above (CGC 8230)

D. Either 1 or 2 (CGC 8230)

QUESTIONS

For services rendered relating to an affidavit or application relating to the securing of a pension (including a Veterans Pension) or the payment of a pension voucher, the notary:
A. may charge $10 for each document.
B. may charge a maximum of $30.
C. shall not charge a fee.
D. none of the above

For administering or certifying an oath of office or for filing or swearing to any claim or demand against any county in the State, a notary:
A. may charge $15 for each document.
B. may charge a maximum of $25.
C. shall not charge a fee.
D. none of the above

Every officer authorized by law to make or give any certificate or other writing is guilty of _____ if he or she makes and delivers as true any certificate or writing containing statements which he or she knows to be false.
A. an infraction
B. a petty offense
C. a misdemeanor
D. a felony

Unless otherwise stated, the time in which any act provided by law is to be done is computed by using calendar days and _____ the first day, and _____ the last, unless the last day is a holiday, and then it is also excluded.
A. excluding ... including
B. excluding ... excluding
C. including ... including
D. including ... excluding

ANSWERS

C. shall not charge any fee. (CGC 6106 and 6107)

C. shall not charge a fee. (CGC 6108)

C. a misdemeanor (CGC 6203) A prosecution for this misdemeanor offense must be commenced (started) within 4 years.

A. excluding … including (CGC 6800)

QUESTIONS

When is a seal not required for acknowledgments?
A. acknowledgment done out of county.
B. acknowledgment done for a non-citizen.
C. acknowledgments on California subdivision maps.
D. None of the above.

A person who is not able to sign his name may sign by using _____.
A. an agent
B. the signature of an employee
C. the signature of his best friend
D. a mark

Which of the following two statements are correct? A notary may take an oral deposition by:
  1) writing it longhand, or
  2) typing it on an electronic device.
A. Only 1 is correct.
B. Only 2 is correct.
C. Both 1 and 2 are not correct.
D. Both 1 and 2 are correct.

If there are two witnesses to the making of the mark, they are _____ to be identified by the notary and are _____ to sign the journal. (Notary Handbook)
A. required …. required
B. required …. not required
C. not required …. not required
D. not required …. required

ANSWERS

C. acknowledgments on California subdivision maps. (The reason is that the surface of these maps doesn't work correctly with ink used for seals.) (CGC section 66436 (c))

D. a mark (Civil Code 14)

D. Both 1 and 2 are correct. (Civil Code 14)

C. not required .... not required (Notary Handbook)

QUESTIONS

A proof of acknowledgment of an instrument may be made before a notary public and all the following, except:
A. a clerk of a superior court
B. a county clerk
C. a retired court administrator
D. a retired judge of a municipal or justice court

A proof of acknowledgment of an instrument may be made before a notary public and all the following, except:
A. an attorney
B. clerk of the board of supervisors
C. a city clerk or a city attorney
D. Secretary of State or Chief Clerk of the Assembly

One section of a notary public journal contains a statement that the type of evidence used to establish the identity of the individual taking the oath or affirmation, or making an acknowledgment, was "_____ evidence."
A. proper
B. correct
C. current
D. satisfactory

A current passport issued by the U.S. does not have to have the description of the person to be acceptable ID.
A. True, only if the passport was issued in the past 4 years.
B. True, in all cases.
C. False. It is not acceptable.
D. none of the above

ANSWERS

C. a retired court administrator (This should read, "A court administrator.") (Civil Code 1181)

A. an attorney (This should read "A district attorney.") (Civil Code 1181)

D. satisfactory (Civil Code 1185)

B. True, in all cases. (California Civil Code 1185(b)(3))

QUESTIONS

If a notary personally knows a signer, is that sufficient to establish the identity of the signer?
A. Yes, if he knows him more than 5 years.
B. No.
C. Yes if the person consents.
D. none of the above

Which of the following choices is not correct? "Satisfactory evidence" means lack of information causing a reasonable person to believe the individual is not the person he claims to be, and:
A. proper ID documents are presented, or
B. the oath of a single credible witness known to notary, or
C. the oaths of two credible witnesses, or
D. the presentation of an original social security card.

"Satisfactory" ID documents must be current or must have been issued within the past 5 years. Qualifying documents include all the following documents, except:
A. An inmate ID card of an inmate still in a California state prison.
B. All driver's licenses issued by any state of the United States.
C. An inmate ID card issued by a sheriff's department if the inmate is in custody of a local detention facility.
D. A United States passport issued 4 years ago.

Acceptable identity documents are current or must have been issued within the past 5 years (and contain a photograph, description of the person, signature of the person, and an identifying number). These documents include all the following, except:
A. An ID card issued by Arizona state.
B. An employee ID card issued by any agency of California.
C. A passport issued by a France (a foreign government).
D. A United States military ID card.

ANSWERS

B. No. (California Civil Code 1185(b))

D. the presentation of an original social security card. This choice is not correct because it is not a part of the "satisfactory evidence" definition. (Civil Code 1185(b)(3) and (4)

B. All driver's licenses issued by any state of the United States. (This is not correct because although a California driver's license is acceptable, a driver's license issued by another state is acceptable ONLY if the license contains a photograph, description of the person, signature of the person, and an identifying number.) (California Civil Code section 1185(b)(4))

C. A passport issued by France (a foreign government). (This is not correct because to be acceptable the passport MUST also have been stamped by the U.S. Immigration and Naturalization Service or the U.S. Citizenship and Immigration Services.) (California Civil Code 1185 (3)(B))

QUESTIONS

A notary public who fails to obtain required satisfactory evidence shall be subject to a civil penalty not exceeding
_____.
A. $750
B. $1,500
C. $2,500
D. $10,000

In addition to establishing the identity of a credible witness (by use of ID documents) the notary must have the credible witness swear or affirm the following, except:
A. The credible witness believes that the person appearing in front of the notary is the signer of the document.
B. The credible witness believes that it is very difficult or impossible for the signer to obtain ID.
C. The credible witness does not personally know the signer.
D. Credible witness does not have financial interest in document.

Which of the following statements is false?
A. A notary public bond is in the amount of $15,000.
B. A notary public commission is 4 years.
C. An acknowledgment is the same as a jurat.
D. A person over the age of 80 is eligible to be a notary public.

If a document is in a foreign language, a notary:
A. cannot notarize the signature on the document.
B. cannot charge a fee.
C. must charge an additional "foreign language fee".
D. can notarize a signature in that document.

ANSWERS

D. $10,000 (Civil Code 1185(b)(B))

C. The credible witness does not personally know the signer. (This is wrong because the credible must swear or affirm that the credible witness **DOES** personally know the signer. (Civil Code section 1185(b)(1)(A)(i)-(v))

C. An acknowledgment is the same as a jurat. (This is not correct.) (Notary Handbook)

D. can notarize a signature in that document. (California Civil Code 1189 and 1195; CGC 8202, 8205 and 8206)

QUESTIONS

The "_____ statement" is part of the Certificate of Acknowledgment. It states the county where the acknowledgment is being made.
A. Location
B. Locality
C. Vendor
D. Venue

If a notary public intentionally (willfully) states to be true a substantial fact that he knows is false, he may be punished with a civil penalty which is not more than $_____.
A. double the amount of his gain.
B. $5,000.
C. $10,000.
D. none of the above

In a certificate of acknowledgment, the notary certifies that he
1) verified the identity of the signer, and that
2) the signer acknowledged signing.
A. 1 only is correct.   C. 1 and 2 are both correct
B. 2 only is correct.   D. 1 and 2 are both incorrect.

A certificate of acknowledgment is executed under the California Civil Code 1189(a)(2) and under penalty of _____.
A. an infraction
B. a petty offense
C. perjury
D. none of the above

ANSWERS

D. Venue (Notary Handbook)

C. $10,000. (Civil Code 1189(a)(2))

C. 1 and 2 are both correct (Civil Code 1189)

C. perjury (California Civil Code 1189(a)(2))

QUESTIONS

Which of the following statements is false?
If a notary completes an acknowledgment that includes statements which the notary is aware are false, the notary:
A. may be liable for administrative action.
B. may charge more than the statutory fee.
C. may be liable for civil penalties.
D. may be guilty of a criminal offense.

The possible penalty for willfully stating as true a material fact that the notary knows to be false in a certificate of acknowledgment is up to and including: _____:
A. $750
B. $1,500
C. $2,500
D. $10,000

If a person (a "principal") has signed a document, but doesn't appear in front of the notary, he can have another person ("_____") appear to prove that the person signed the document.
A. "subscribing witness"   C. a "juror"
B. a "next friend"   D. none of the above

If a law requires that a signature be notarized, the requirement is satisfied with respect to an electronic signature if an electronic record includes, in addition to the electronic signature to be notarized, the _____ signature of a notary public.
A. certified   C. original
B. electronic   D. none of the above

ANSWERS

B. may charge more than the statutory fee. (A notary CANNOT notarize such a document and CANNOT charge a fee. (Civil Code 1189(a)(2))

D. $10,000 (California Civil Code 1189(a)(2))

A. "subscribing witness" (Code of Civil Procedure 1935)

B. electronic (Civil Code 1633.11)

QUESTIONS

If the last day for the performance of any act provided or required by law to be performed within a specified period of time is a holiday, then that period is hereby extended to and including _____.
A. the holiday.
B. the next day that is a holiday.
C. the day before the holiday
D. the next day that is not a holiday.

A _____ witness is one who sees a writing executed or hears it acknowledged, and at the request of the party thereupon signs his name as a witness.
A. sworn
B. subscribing
C. verifiable
D. none of the above

When administering an oath, the following are required:
A. The person and the notary must both be standing.
B. The person and the notary must both be sitting.
C. The person must be over the age of 40.
D. None of the above.

If a copy of a power of attorney is certified by a notary, the power of attorney:
A. is null and void.
B. is illegal.
C. has the same force as the original power of attorney.
D. none of the above

ANSWERS

D. the next day that is not a holiday. (Code of Civil Procedure 12a)

B. subscribing (Code of Civil Procedure 1935)

D. None of the above. (Code of Civil Procedure 2094)

C. has the same force as the original power of attorney. (Probate Code 4307)

QUESTIONS

Can a notary public perform marriage ceremonies?
A. Yes, in all cases.
B. Yes if the notary is a priest, rabbi, or minister.
C. No unless the notary pays the required licensing fee.
D. No, in all cases.

What is the title of the official who can authorize a notary public to issue confidential marriage licenses?
A. the California Secretary of State
B. the California Governor
C. the county clerk
D. none of the above

Which of the following choices is correct?
A notary public application may be denied due to:
A. the applicant being over the age of 62.
B. non-compliance with family support obligations.
C. the applicant being unable to provide a surety bond greater than $15,000.
D. none of the above

Which of the following four statements is most correct? An applicant for notary public commission:
A. must pass a background check.
B. generally, must be a legal resident of the State of California.
C. must submit a 2-inch x 2-inch color photo.
D. must submit all the above.

ANSWERS

B. Yes if the notary is a priest, rabbi, or minister. (Family Code 400 to 402)

C. the county clerk (in the county of residence of the notary public). (Family Code 530)

B. non-compliance with family support obligations. (Family Code 8220)

D. must submit all the above. (Notary Handbook)

QUESTIONS

Choose the best answer: An application for notary public commission may be denied by the Secretary of State for any of the following reasons:
A. only for conviction of a felony.
B. only for conviction of a lesser included offense.
C. only for conviction for a felony or any lesser included offense.
D. failure to disclose any conviction, or a conviction for a felony or conviction of a disqualifying lesser included offense.

A notary public bond:
A. is in the amount of $20,000.
B. is an insurance policy for the notary public.
C. is not required for a notary who is being reappointed.
D. does not remove the personal liability of a notary for claims against the notary.

"Satisfactory evidence" includes:
A. proper identification documents.
B. the oath of a single credible witness.
C. the oaths of two credible witnesses.
D. all the above

Which of the following forms is the most frequently completed form by a notary public?
A. a jurat
B. a deposition
C. an acknowledgment
D. none of the above

ANSWERS

D. failure to disclose any conviction, or a conviction for a felony or conviction of a disqualifying lesser included offense. (Notary Handbook)

D. does not remove the personal liability of a notary for claims against the notary. (Notary Handbook)

D. all the above (Notary Handbook)

C. an acknowledgment (Notary Handbook)

QUESTIONS

Can a notary complete a certificate of acknowledgment that will be used in another state?
A. Yes, in all cases.
B. No, in all cases.
C. Yes if the form doesn't include a determination or certification by the notary of the signer's representative capacity or other notarial conclusions prohibited by California law.
D. none of the above

A notary public does not have a financial interest in a transaction if he is acting in any of the following capacities for a person having a direct financial interest in the transaction:
A. escrow holder
B. agent, employee
C. insurer, attorney
D. all the above

Which of the following statements is not correct? When completing a jurat, the notary certifies that:
A. the signer appeared personally before the notary,
B. the signer signed the document in front of the notary on the date indicated,
C. the signer is over the age of 21.
D. the notary administered the affirmation or oath.

Is there a prescribed wording for an oath?
A. Yes. It must be used in all cases.
B. Yes. It is required to be used only in all notarial forms relating to real property.
C. Yes. The prescribed wording is available in all languages.
D. No. There is no prescribed wording for the oath.

ANSWERS

C. Yes, if the form doesn't include a determination or certification by the notary of the signer's representative capacity or other notarial conclusions prohibited by California law. (Notary Handbook)

D. all the above (Notary Handbook)

C. the signer is over the age of 21. (Notary Handbook)

D. No. There is no prescribed wording for the oath. (There are only "acceptable" oaths such as, "Do you swear or affirm that the statements in this document are true?") (Notary Handbook)

CALIFORNIA NOTARY PUBLIC / 177

QUESTIONS

(Proof of execution by a subscribing witness): Among other things, the subscribing witness swears (says under oath) that:
1. the person who signed the document is in fact the person described in the document, and
2. the subscribing witness personally knows the person who signed the document.
A. 1 only is correct.   C. 1 and 2 are both correct.
B. 2 only is correct.   D. 1 and 2 are both not correct.

A notary can notarize the signature on a document which has to do with citizenship or immigration. However, a notary cannot suggest the information to be placed in the document, or help a person fill out the documents, except for the
_____.
A. affidavit
B. police report
C. criminal history
D. date and signature

The signer by mark is required to write the mark in the notary journal. Also, the making of the mark must be witnessed by _____ people. One of the two persons must write next to the mark the name of the person making the mark. However, the ___ witnesses are not required to sign the notary journal.
A. 2 2
B. 3 3
C. 4 4
D. No witness is required if the mark is made before the notary.

The notary must identify the person making a mark by:
1. examination of the mark, and
2. satisfactory evidence.
A. 1 only is correct.   C. 1 and 2 are both correct.
B. 2 only is correct.   D. 1 and 2 are both not correct.

ANSWERS

C. 1 and 2 are both correct. (Notary Handbook)

D. date and signature. (Notary Handbook)

A. 2 .... 2 (The two witnesses are not required to sign the notary journal or be identified by the notary.) (Notary Handbook)

B. 2 only is correct. (Notary Handbook)

<u>QUESTIONS</u>

The maker of a mark:
A. must be able to speak English.
B. must be a US citizen.
C. must make the mark with red ink.
D. none of the above.

When a notary is asked to notarize a signature in a document in a foreign language:
A. the notary must refuse to do so, in all cases.
B. the notary may do so because he is only notarizing the signature.
C. the notary may use an interpreter.
D. none of the above

Jane Barret is a California Notary Public. Her best friend asks her to notarize a document for her. Can Jane Barret notarize the document without asking for her friend's proof of identity?
A. Yes, because she knows the person personally.
B. Yes if her friend pays the $10 fee.
C. No. She must ask and obtain satisfactory evidence before she can notarize the document.
D. Yes if her friend is over the age of 21.

The submission of fingerprints by notary public applicants is required:
A. only for the first time a person applies for the notary public commission.
B. every time a person applies for a notary public commission, even if the person held a previous commission.
C. only if the person has been convicted of a misdemeanor or felony.
D. only if the person has been convicted of an infraction,

ANSWERS

D. none of the above. (Notary Handbook)

B. the notary may do so because he is only notarizing the signature. Notary Handbook)

C. No. She must ask and obtain satisfactory evidence before she can notarize the document. (Notary Handbook)

B. every time a person applies for a notary public commission, even if the person held a previous commission. (Notary Handbook)

QUESTIONS

What is the title of the California State official who determines whether a conviction is "disqualifying" for a person to become a notary public?
A. the Governor
B. the State Comptroller
C. the Secretary of State
D. the County Clerk

If a new applicant fails to file the oath and bond on time:
A. the commission will not be valid.
B. he must pay a $500 fine.
C. he must pay a $50 fee.
D. none of the above.

Which of the following two statements are correct?
1. For a notary to complete a jurat based on ID documents, the person must appear and sign the document in the presence of the notary, and 2. For the notary to prepare an acknowledgment, the signer must appear before the notary and acknowledge that the signer executed the document, NOT that it was signed in the presence of the notary.
A. 1 only is correct.   C. 1 and 2 are both correct.
B. 2 only is correct.   D. 1 and 2 are both not correct.

A notary may resign his commission by:
A. publishing a notice in a daily newspaper.
B. posting a sign in his office.
C. sending a letter of resignation to the Secretary of State.
D. none of the above.

ANSWERS

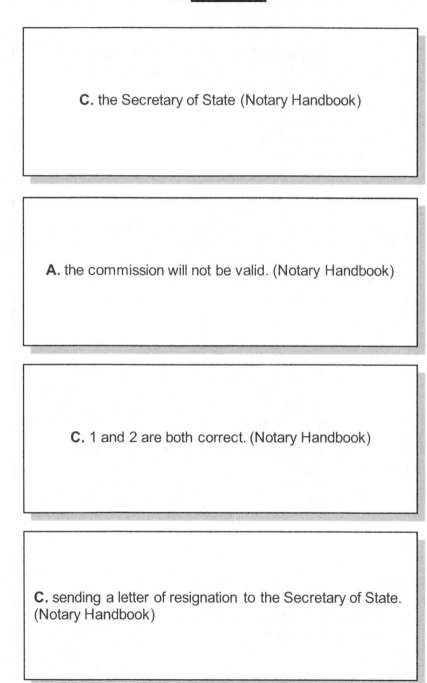

C. the Secretary of State (Notary Handbook)

A. the commission will not be valid. (Notary Handbook)

C. 1 and 2 are both correct. (Notary Handbook)

C. sending a letter of resignation to the Secretary of State. (Notary Handbook)

QUESTIONS

A notary public can certify:
A. copies of birth and death records.
B. copies of marriage records.
C. copies of fetal death records.
D. none of the above

Which of the following is correct?
A. A notary public may practice law in certain cases.
B. All notaries public may advertise that they practice law.
C. A notary public may give legal advice if he wishes.
D. A notary public is prohibited from practicing law unless he is a licensed California attorney.

For filing a forged document with the county recorder (single-family residence with not more than four dwelling units) the penalty may include a fine not exceeding
_____.
A. $25,000
B. $35,000
C. $50,000
D. $75,000

A person making a false statement to a notary regarding single-family residence with not more than four dwelling units is guilty of a(n) _____.
A. infraction
B. misdemeanor
C. felony
D. civil misconduct

ANSWERS

D. none of the above (These records can only be certified by designated public officials such as the State and local Registrars.) (Health and Safety Code 103545)

D. A notary public is prohibited from practicing law unless he is a licensed California attorney. (CGC section 8214.1(g); California Business and Professions Code section 6215)

D. $75,000 (Penal Code 115.5)

C. felony (Penal Code 115.5(b))

QUESTIONS

A person who forges a seal or handwriting is guilty of
_____, punishable by imprisonment.
A. perjury
B. forgery
C. bribery
D. harassment

A person under oath who willfully states as true any
material matter which he knows to be false, is guilty of

_____.
A. perjury
B. forgery
C. bribery
D. harassment

Perjury is punishable by a term of imprisonment in a State
jail for _____.
A. 3 months
B. 9 months
C. two, three, or four years
D. none of the above

"It does no matter how slowly you go as long as you do not
stop."
       Confucius

ANSWERS

B. forgery (Penal Code 473)

A. perjury (Penal Code 118)

C. two, three, or four years (Penal Code 126)

"If you dream it, you can do it."
Walt Disney

PRACTICE EXAM 1

1. What is the title of the California official who appoints notaries and prescribes the written examination that applicants must pass?
A. Governor
C. Secretary of State
B. Attorney General
D. State Controller

-----

2. When a notary executes a jurat, the affiant must:
A. pay a fee of $25.
B. sign the document in front of the notary.
C. be accompanied by three witnesses.
D. none of the above

-----

3. A notarial certificate:
A. must be in a foreign language that is the same as the language of the document.
B. may be in English or a foreign language.
C. must be in English.
D. must be in the language preferred by the person signing the document.

-----

4. Choose the best answer: A notary public employed by a financial institution is empowered during his employment to:
A. demand acceptance and payment of foreign and inland bills of exchange.
B. exercise powers the laws of other states and countries permit a notary to perform.
C. Neither A nor B.
D. Both A and B.

-----

5. Which of the following is authorized to have access to the notary journal without the notary being present?
A. an employee of the notary
B. the employer of the notary

C. a trusted and mature family member
D. no one

-----

6. If there are one or two credible witnesses used to establish identity, which of the credible witnesses must sign the notary journal?
A. There is a requirement for signature only if there is one credible witness.
B. There is a requirement for signatures only if there are two credible witnesses.
C. In both cases there is no requirement for signatures.
D. The credible witnesses must sign the journal whether there are one or two credible witnesses.

-----

7. Which of the following statements regarding a notary public journal is not correct?
A. The notary must keep one or more active journals at a time.
B. The notary must record in the journal all notarial acts performed.
C. The acts recorded in the journal must be in sequential order.
D. The journal must be kept in a secure area. It must also be under the exclusive control of the notary.

-----

8. If a member of the public requests in writing a copy of a transaction recorded in the journal, the notary must respond within ___ business days and may charge thirty cents ($.30) per copy page.
A. 10
B. 15
C. 20
D. 30

-----

9. If a notary public commission is no longer valid, the seal:
A. must be stored in a secure place.
B. may only be used for 30 more days.

C. must be destroyed.
D. none of the above.

-----

10. A notary public seal shall not be duplicated, sold, manufactured, or offered for sale without the authorization by the _____.
A. county clerk
B. county court
C. Secretary of State
D. State Comptroller

-----

11. The maximum fee for taking an acknowledgment or proof of a deed, or other instrument, to include the seal and the writing of the certificate is _____ for each signature taken.
A. $5
B. $15
C. $17
D. $20

-----

12. The maximum fee that may be charged to notarize signatures on vote by mail ballot identification envelopes or other voting materials is _____.
A. $2
B. $5
C. $10
D. No fee is permitted to be charged.

-----

13. The maximum fee for an acknowledgment or proof of a deed (or other instrument, including the seal and writing the certificate) is _____.
A. $10
B. $15
C. $20
D. none of the above

14. After a notary public commission is issued, the person has ___ days to 1) file an oath of office with the clerk of county, and 2) file a surety bond with the office of the clerk of county.

A. 10 days
B. 20 days
C. 30 days
D. 60 days

-----

15. Willful failure to notify the Secretary of State of a change of address shall be punishable as an infraction by a fine of not more than _____.

A. $100
B. $500
C. $1,000
D. $1,500

-----

16. Grounds for refusal, revocation, or suspension of notary public commission do not include:

A. Securing the sequential journal.
B. Failure to pay a judgment demanded by Secretary of State.
C. Willful failure to provide access to the journal after a demand by a peace officer.
D. Charging more than the statutory fees.

-----

17. The civil penalty for failure to obtain a required thumbprint in a sequential journal is an amount not exceeding $_____.

A. $500
B. $1,000
C. $1,500
D. $2,500

-----

18. Generally, can a notary public notarize a document if he has a financial interest in the document?

A. Yes, in all cases.
B. Yes if he does not charge a notarial fee.
C. Yes if he is requested to do so.
D. None of the above.

19. If a notary public intentionally (willfully) surrenders his seal to a person not authorized by law to have it, or if the notary fails to secure his journal, he is guilty of:
A. an infraction
B. a petty offense
C. a misdemeanor
D. a felony

-----

20. A notary can certify copies of the following vital records:
A. birth certificates.
B. marriage certificates.
C. death certificates.
D. none of the above

-----

21. Unless otherwise stated, the time in which any act provided by law is to be done is computed by using calendar days and _____ the first day, and _____ the last, unless the last day is a holiday, and then it is also excluded.
A. excluding ... including
B. excluding ... excluding
C. including ... including
D. including ... excluding

-----

22. A proof of acknowledgment of an instrument may be made before a notary public and all the following, except:
A. an attorney
B. a clerk of the board of supervisors
C. a city clerk or a city attorney
D. Secretary of State or Chief Clerk of the Assembly

-----

23. "Satisfactory" ID documents must be current or must have been issued within the past 5 years. Qualifying documents include all the following documents, except:
A. An inmate ID card of an inmate still in a California state prison.

B. All driver's licenses issued by any state of the United States.
C. A form of inmate ID card issued by a sheriff's department if the inmate is in custody of a local detention facility.
D. A United States passport issued 4 years ago.

-----

24. If a document is in a foreign language, a notary:
A. cannot notarize the signature on the document.
B. cannot charge a fee.
C. must charge an additional "foreign language fee."
D. can notarize a signature in that document.

-----

25. The possible penalty for willfully stating as true a material fact that the notary knows to be false in a certificate of acknowledgment is up to and including: _____.
A. $750
B. $1,500
C. $2,500
D. $10,000

-----

26. If a copy of a power of attorney is certified by a notary, the power of attorney:
A. is null and void.
B. is illegal.
C. has the same force as the original power of attorney.
D. none of the above

-----

27. Which of the following forms is the most frequently completed form by a notary public?
A. a jurat
B. a deposition
C. an acknowledgment
D. none of the above

28. A notary can notarize the signature on a document which has to do with citizenship or immigration. However, a notary cannot suggest the information to be placed in the document, or help a person fill out the documents, except for the
_____.
A. affidavit
B. police report
C. criminal history
D. date and signature

-----

29. What is the title of the California State official who determines whether a conviction is "disqualifying" for a person to become a notary public?
A. the Governor
B. the State Comptroller
C. the Secretary of State
D. the County Clerk

-----

30. A notary public can certify:
A. copies of birth and death records.
B. copies of marriage records.
C. copies of fetal death records.
D. none of the above

PRACTICE EXAM 1
ANSWERS

1. **C.** Secretary of State (CGC 8200)

2. **B.** sign the document in front of the notary. (CGC 8202)

3. **C.** must be in English. (California Civil Code 1188, 1189 and 1195; CGC 8202)

4. **D.** Both A and B. (CGC 8205)

5. **D.** no one (CGC 8206(a)(1))

6. **D.** The credible witnesses must sign the journal whether there are one or two credible witnesses. (CGC 8206(a)(E)

7. **A.** The notary must keep one or more active journals at a time. (This is NOT correct because ONLY ONE journal may be kept active at any one time. (CGC 8206(a))

8. **B.** 15 business days (CGC 8206(c) and 8206.5) Note that it is 15 BUSINESS days (and NOT 15 calendar days.)

9. **C.** must be destroyed. (CGC 8207)

10. **C.** Secretary of State (CGC 8207.2) (Willful violation may be punished by fine not to exceed $1,500.)

11. **B.** $15 (CGC 8211)

12. **D.** No fee is permitted to be charged. (CGC 8211)

13. **D.** none of the above (CGC 8211) ($15 for each signature.)

14. **C.** 30 days (CGC 8213)

15. **B.** $500 (CGC 8213.6)

16. **A.** Securing the sequential journal. (CGC 8214.1 (o))

17. **D.** $2,500 (CGC 8214.23)

18. **D.** None of the above. (Generally, the notary cannot notarize documents in which he has a beneficial or financial interest.) (CGC 8224)

19. **C.** a misdemeanor (CGC 8228.1) (If a notary public

intentionally (willfully) surrenders his seal to a person not authorized by law to have it, or the notary fails to secure his journal, he is guilty of a **misdemeanor**.)

20. **D.** none of the above (CGC 8230)

21. **A.** excluding … including (CGC 6800)

22. **A.** an attorney (This should read "A district attorney.") (Civil Code 1181)

23. **B.** All driver's licenses issued by any state of the United States. (This is not correct because although a California driver's license is acceptable, a driver's license issued by another state is acceptable ONLY if the license contains a photograph, description of the person, signature of the person, and an identifying number.) (California Civil Code section 1185(b)(4))

24. **D.** can notarize a signature in that document. (California Civil Code 1189 and 1195; CGC 8202, 8205 and 8206)

25. **D.** $10,000 (California Civil Code 1189(a)(2))

26. **C.** has the same force as the original power of attorney. (Probate Code 4307)

27. **C.** an acknowledgment (Notary Handbook)

28. **D.** date and signature. (Notary Handbook)

29. **C.** the Secretary of State (Notary Handbook)

30. **D.** none of the above (These records can only be certified by designated public officials such as the State and local Registrars.) (Health and Safety Code 103545)

PRACTICE EXAM 2

1. Everyone who wishes to apply for appointment as a California notary public must be at least ___ years of age.
A. 35
B. 24
C. 21
D. 18

2. A person must appear before a notary for the following:
   1. an acknowledgment
   2. a jurat
A. 1 only
B. 2 only
C. both 1 and 2
D. neither 1 nor 2

-----

3. A private employer and a notary may agree that the notary during his employment:
A. charge greater than the maximum fee.
B. the notary may perform only notarial services for transactions directly connected to the business.
C. charge double the statutory fee.
D. none of the above.

-----

4. If a check by notary public applicant in payment for the commission, application, examination, and fingerprint report is not accepted by the bank, the Secretary of State may:
A. fine the applicant $100.
B. reduce the applicant's score on the notary public written examination by 10 points.
C. cancel the commission.
D. none of the above

-----

5. If a police officer seizes a notary public journal, the notary shall notify the Secretary of State by certified mail within _____.

A. 5 days
B. 10 days
C. 15 days
D. 30 days

-----

6. Which of the following is not correct?
The notary journal must contain:
A. the date, time, and type of each notarial act.
B. the character of every instrument that is acknowledged.
C. the signature of each person whose signature is being
   notarized.
D. the signatures of all persons who witness the making of a
   mark that is being notarized.

-----

7. Which one of the following four choices lists an item that is
not required to be included in a notary public journal?
A. Date and time of every official notarial act
B. The type of each official act (Example: jurat)
C. The signature and address of the person(s) whose signature
   is being notarized.
D. A statement that "satisfactory evidence" was used to identify
   the person taking the oath (or making an acknowledgment).

-----

8. Which of the following four choices is not correct? A notary
must surrender his journal:
A. when required by law.
B. to a peace officer who believes the journal has evidence of a
   criminal offense.
C. upon request of the county clerk where the notary
   commission is filed.
D. to his employer if the employer requests the journal.

-----

9. Which of the following statements regarding a notary public
seal is not correct?
A. The seal must be photographically reproducible.

B. In addition to the notary rubber stamp, a notary may not use an embosser seal.
C. The seal must contain the words "Notary Public."
D. The seal must contain the name of the notary public (which must be the same as on the notary public commission).

-----

10. Which of the following statements is not correct?
A. A sequential journal shall not be surrendered to an employer when the notary ends his employment.
B. A notary public who intentionally (willfully) does not maintain his journal properly is guilty of a felony.
C. If notary commission is no longer valid, notary must deliver all notarial records and journal(s) to the clerk of county.
D. The records cited in "C" must be delivered within 30 days.

-----

11. The maximum fee for administering an oath or affirmation to one person and executing the jurat, including the seal is _____.
A. $2
B. $5
C. $10
D. $15

-----

12. The fee to submit an address change form or address change letter is _____.
A. $10
B. $15
C. $20
D. none of the above

-----

13. Grounds for refusal, revocation, or suspension of notary public commission do not include:
A. Substantial misstatement in notary application.
B. Conviction of an infraction.
C. Denial of a professional license due to dishonesty.
D. Failure to faithfully discharge duties of a notary public.

14. Which of the following is not a correct maximum civil penalty for the stated offense committed by a notary?
A. dishonesty, fraud, deceit: $1,500
B. misleading advertising by a notary: $750
C. charging more than the maximum allowable fees: $750
D. failure to complete acknowledgment at proper time: $1,500

-----

15. When advertising in the Spanish language, can a notary translate "Notary Public" as "notario publico"?
A. Yes, if the periodical is published by a non-profit group.
B. No. He is prohibited from doing so.
C. Yes if the periodical is entirely in the Spanish language.
D. none of the above

-----

16. A person who holds himself out to be a notary but is not a notary is guilty of _____.
A. an infraction
B. a misdemeanor
C. a felony
D. civil contempt

-----

17. If a notary intentionally does not properly maintain his notary journal, he is guilty of _____.
A. an infraction
B. a misdemeanor
C. a felony
D. none of the above

-----

18. Generally, if a notary executes a jurat and the document contains the identity of the affiant and age (including the birthdate), the notary shall require verification of the birthdate or age by either:
1. A certified copy of the person's birth certificate, or
2. An identification card or driver's license issued by the Department of Motor Vehicles.

A. 1 only   C. Neither 1 nor 2
B. 2 only   D. Either 1 or 2

-----

19. A person who is not able to sign his name may sign by using
_____.
A. an agent
B. the signature of an employee
C. the signature of his best friend
D. a mark

-----

20. One section of a notary public journal contains a statement that the type of evidence used to establish the identity of the individual taking the oath or affirmation, or making an acknowledgment, was "_____ evidence."
A. proper
B. correct
C. current
D. satisfactory

-----

21. Acceptable identity documents are current or must have been issued within the past 5 years (and contain a photograph, description of the person, signature of the person, and an identifying number). These documents include all the following, except:
A. An ID card issued by Arizona state.
B. An employee ID card issued by any agency of California.
C. A passport issued by a France (a foreign government).
D. A United States military ID card.

-----

22. If a notary public intentionally (willfully) states to be true a substantial fact that he knows is false, he may be punished with a civil penalty which is not more than $_____.
A. double the amount of his gain.
B. $5,000.
C. $10,000.

D. none of the above

-----

23. If a law requires that a signature be notarized, the requirement is satisfied with respect to an electronic signature if an electronic record includes, in addition to the electronic signature to be notarized, the _____ signature of a notary public.
A. certified   C. original
B. electronic   D. none of the above

-----

24. What is the title of the official who can authorize a notary public to issue confidential marriage licenses?
A. the California Secretary of State
B. the California Governor
C. the county clerk
D. none of the above

-----

25. Which of the following four statements is most correct? An applicant for notary public commission:
A. must pass a background check.
B. generally, must be a legal resident of the State of California.
C. must submit a 2-inch x 2-inch color photo.
D. must submit all the above.

-----

26. A notary public does not have a financial interest in a transaction if he is acting in any of the following capacities for a person having a direct financial interest in the transaction:
A. escrow holder
B. agent, employee
C. insurer, attorney
D. all the above

-----

27. The notary must identify the person making a mark by:
1. examination of the mark, and

2. satisfactory evidence.

A. 1 only is correct.
B. 2 only is correct.

C. 1 and 2 are both correct.
D. 1 and 2 are both not correct.

-----

28. Which of the following two statements are correct?
1. For the notary to complete a jurat based on identification documents of the signer, the person must appear and sign the document in the presence of the notary.
2. For the notary to prepare an acknowledgment, the signer must appear before the notary and acknowledge that the signer executed the document, NOT that it was signed in the presence of the notary.

A. 1 only is correct.
B. 2 only is correct.

C. 1 and 2 are both correct.
D. 1 and 2 are both not correct.

-----

29. Which of the following is correct?
A. A notary public may practice law in certain cases.
B. All notaries public may advertise that they practice law.
C. A notary public may give legal advice if he wishes.
D. A notary public is prohibited from practicing law unless he is a licensed California attorney.

-----

30. Perjury is punishable by a term of imprisonment in a State jail for _____.
A. 3 months
B. 9 months
C. two, three, or four years
D. none of the above

PRACTICE EXAM 2
ANSWERS

1. **D.** 18 (CGC sections 8201)
2. **B.** 2 only (for a jurat) (Civil Code 1189 and CGC 8202)
3. **B.** notary may perform only notarial services for transactions directly connected to the business. (CGC 8202.7)
4. **C.** cancel the commission. (CGC 8204.1)
5. **B.** 10 days (CGC 8206 (d))
6. **D.** the signatures of all persons who witness the making of a mark that is being notarized. (This is not a requirement of CGC 8206. Also, in the law relating to making of a mark in front of a notary, the signatures of the witnesses are specifically stated as NOT required.)
7. **C.** The signature and address of the person(s) whose signature is being notarized. (This statement is NOT correct because the addresses of the persons are NOT required to be recorded in the notary public journal. (CGC 8206(a))
8. **D.** to his employer, if the employer requests the journal. (The notary is prohibited from surrendering his journal to his employer.) (CGC 8206(d))
9. **B.** In addition to the rubber stamp, a notary may not use an embosser seal. (This statement is not correct because the notary **MAY** use an embosser seal in addition to the rubber seal.) (CGC 8207)
10. **B.** Notary who intentionally (willfully) does not maintain his journal is guilty of a felony. (NOT correct because a notary public who intentionally (willfully) does not maintain his journal is guilty of a MISDEMEANOR.) (CGC 8209)
11. **D.** $15 (CGC 8211)

12. **D.** none of the above (NO fee required.) (CGC 8213)

13. **B.** Conviction of an infraction. (This should read, "Conviction of a <u>felony</u>.") (CGC 8214.1 (b))

14. **B.** misleading advertising by a notary: $750 (The correct maximum civil penalty is $1,500.) (CGC 8214.15)

15. **B.** No. He is prohibited from doing so. (CGC 8219.5)

16. **B.** a misdemeanor (CGC 8227.1)

17. **B.** a misdemeanor (CGC 8228.1)

18. **D.** Either 1 or 2 (CGC 8230)

19. **D.** a mark (Civil Code 14)

20. **D.** satisfactory (Civil Code 1185)

21. **C.** A passport issued by France (a foreign government). (This is not correct because to be acceptable the passport MUST also have been stamped by the U.S. Immigration and Naturalization Service or U.S. Citizenship and Immigration Services.) (California Civil Code 1185 (3)(B))

22. **C.** $10,000. (Civil Code 1189(a)(2))

23. **B.** electronic (Civil Code 1633.11)

24. **C.** the county clerk (in the county of residence of the notary public). (Family Code 530)

25. **D.** must submit all the above. (Notary Handbook)

26. **D.** all the above (Notary Handbook)

27. **B.** 2 only is correct. (Notary Handbook)

28. **C.** 1 and 2 are both correct. (Notary Handbook)

29. **D.** A notary public is prohibited from practicing law unless he is a licensed California attorney. (CGC section 8214.1(g)) California Business and Professions Code section 6215)

30. **C.** two, three, or four years (Penal Code 126)

PRACTICE EXAM 3

1. In addition to passing the notary public written examination, an applicant must submit his fingerprints within _____ to be used in his background check.
A. 30 days   C. 6 months
B. 3 months   D. one year

-----

2. Which of the following two statements are correct? A notary public can complete a jurat:
1. that was mailed to him, but where the person did not appear before the notary.
2. that was mailed to him by a person the notary knows personally, even though the person did not appear before the notary.
A. 1 only is correct.   C. 1 and 2 are both incorrect.
B. 2 only is correct.   D. 1 and 2 are both correct.

-----

3. A notary public appointed for a military reservation must charge:
A. the minimum fees.
B. the maximum fees.
C. no fees.
D. none of the above.

-----

4. Grounds for denial, revocation, or suspension of appointment and commission include all the following, except:
A. charging more than the statutory fee.
B. conviction of a felony.
C. failure to submit to the Secretary of State requested documents.
D. securing the official journal and seal.

-----

5. Which of the following ID information is not required to be recorded in the notary journal?

A. the type of identifying document (Example: passport)
B. the serial or other identifying number of the ID document
C. the date of issue or the date of expiration of the ID document
D. the physical condition of the ID document

-----

6. Which of the following four choices is not correct? If a notary public journal is damaged or rendered unusable, etc., the notary must inform the Secretary of State by certified or registered mail and include the following information:
A. the notary public commission number
B. the commission expiration date
C. a copy of the police report
D. the time periods of the journal entries

-----

7. When a notary surrenders his journal to a peace officer, he must obtain a receipt. The notary is also required to notify the Secretary of State within _____ by certified mail.
A. 5 days
B. 10 days
C. 15 days
D. 20 days

-----

8. Which of the following statements regarding a notary public seal is not correct?
A. The seal may be circular (not over two inches).
B. The seal may be rectangular (not more than 1 inch in width by 2 and ½ inches in length.)
C. The seal must have serrated edge (or milled edge border).
D. The seal cannot be a rubber stamp seal.

-----

9. If the employee notary (of a public employer) resigns or is terminated, this is considered:
A. the same as a renewal of the commission of the notary.
B. the same as a temporary suspension of the notary public commission.

C. the same as having been found guilty of a misdemeanor.
D. the same as a resignation of the commission of the notary.

-----

10. The maximum fee for all services rendered in connection with taking a deposition: $_____, and in addition: $_____ for administering the oath to the witness, and $_____ for the certificate to the deposition.
A. $10 .... $10 .... $10
B. $20 .... $10 .... $10
C. $30 .... $7 ...... $7
D. none of the above

-----

11. The maximum fee that may be charged to a United States military veteran for notarization of an application or a claim for a pension, allotment, allowance, compensation, insurance, or any other veteran's benefit is _____.
A. $2
B. $5
C. $10
D. No fee is permitted to be charged.

-----

12. A change of address by the notary must be reported to _____ within 30 days by certified mail.
A. county clerk
B. Secretary of State.
C. the State Comptroller.
D. the county court.

-----

13. Grounds for refusal, revocation, or suspension of notary public commission do not include:
A. Commission of any act involving dishonesty.
B. Failure to complete an acknowledgment timely.
C. Failure to administer a required oath.
D. Unknowingly executing a false certificate.

14. Performing a fraudulent notarial act relating to a deed of trust (real property not more than four dwelling units) is a:
A. infraction.
B. misdemeanor.
C. felony.
D. none of the above

-----

15. A person who intentionally destroys notary public records belonging to a notary is guilty of:
A. an infraction.
B. a misdemeanor.
C. a felony.
D. none of the above

-----

16. For administering or certifying an oath of office or for filing or swearing to any claim or demand against any county in the State, a notary:
A. may charge $15 for each document.
B. may charge a maximum of $25.
C. shall not charge a fee.
D. none of the above

-----

17. If there are two witnesses to the making of the mark, they are (required? / not required?) to be identified by the notary and are (required? / not required?) to sign the journal. (Notary Handbook)
A. required .... required
B. required .... not required
C. not required .... not required
D. not required .... required

-----

18. If a notary personally knows a signer, is that sufficient to establish the identity of the signer?
A. Yes, if he knows him more than 5 years.
B. No.

C. Yes if the person consents.
D. none of the above

-----

19. In addition to establishing the identity of a credible witness (by use of ID documents) the notary must have the credible witness swear or affirm the following, except:
A. The credible witness believes that the person appearing in front of the notary is the signer of the document.
B. The credible witness believes that it is difficult or impossible for the signer to obtain ID.
C. The credible witness does not personally know the signer.
D. The credible witness does not have any financial interest in the document.

-----

20. A certificate of acknowledgment is executed under the California Civil Code 1189(a)(2) penalty of _____.
A. an infraction
B. a petty offense
C. perjury
D. none of the above

-----

21. A _____ witness is one who sees a writing executed or hears it acknowledged, and at the request of the party thereupon signs his name as a witness.
A. sworn
B. subscribing
C. verifiable
D. none of the above

-----

22. What is the title of the official who can authorize a notary public to issue confidential marriage licenses?
A. the California Secretary of State
B. the California Governor
C. the county clerk
D. none of the above

23. A notary public bond:
A. is in the amount of $20,000.
B. is an insurance policy for the notary public.
C. is not required for a notary who is being reappointed.
D. does not remove the personal liability of a notary for claims against the notary.

-----

24. A notary public does not have a financial interest in a transaction if he is acting in any of the following capacities for a person having a direct financial interest in the transaction:
A. escrow holder
B. agent, employee
C. insurer, attorney
D. all the above

-----

25. Is there a prescribed wording for an oath?
A. Yes. It must be used in all cases.
B. Yes. It is required to be used only in all notarial forms relating to real property.
C. Yes. The prescribed wording is available in all languages.
D. No. There is no prescribed wording for the oath.

-----

26. When a notary is asked to notarize a signature in a document in a foreign language:
A. the notary must refuse to do so, in all cases.
B. the notary may do so because he is only notarizing the signature.
C. the notary may use an interpreter.
D. none of the above

-----

27. For filing a forged document with the county recorder (single-family residence with not more than four dwelling units) the penalty may include a fine not exceeding _____.
A. $25,000
B. $35,000
C. $50,000
D. $75,000

-----

28. A notary may resign his commission by:
A. publishing a notice in a daily newspaper.
B. posting a sign in his office.
C. sending a letter of resignation to the Secretary of State.
D. none of the above.

-----

29. Which of the following is correct?
A. A notary public may practice law in certain cases.
B. All notaries public may advertise that they practice law.
C. A notary public may give legal advice if he wishes.
D. A notary public is prohibited from practicing law unless he is a licensed California attorney.

-----

30. A person making a false statement to a notary regarding single-family residence with not more than four dwelling units is guilty of a(n) _____. (California Penal Code 115.5(b))
A. infraction
B. misdemeanor
C. felony
D. civil misconduct

PRACTICE EXAM 3
ANSWERS

1. **D.** one year (CGC 8201.1(a)

2. **C.** Numbers 1 and 2 are both incorrect. (The person MUST personally appear before the notary public.) (CGC 8202)

3. **C.** no fees. (CGC 8203.6)

4. **D.** securing the official journal and seal. (This should read, "FAILURE to secure the official journal and seal.) (CGC 8205, 8214.1, 8219.5, and 8223).

5. **D.** the <u>physical condition</u> of the ID document (This is not correct because it is not one of the items listed in CGC 8206(a)(2)(D))

6. **C.** a copy of the police report (This is NOT correct because a copy of the police report must be included WHEN APPLICABLE, usually when an offense has been committed, and not when damaged due to negligence.) (CGC 8206(b))

7. **B.** 10 days (CGC 8206(d))

8. **D.** The seal cannot be a rubber stamp seal. (This statement is not correct because the seal **MAY** be a rubber stamp seal.) (CGC 8207)

9. **D.** the same as a resignation of the commission of the notary. (CGC 8200)

10. **C.** $30 …. $7 …… $7 (CGC 8211)

11. **D.** No fee is permitted to be charged. (CGC 8211)

12. **B.** Secretary of State. (No fee is required for filing an address change.) (CGC 8213.5)

13. **D.** Unknowingly executing a false certificate. (Should read, "<u>Knowingly</u> executing a false certificate.") (CGC 8214.1 (I))

14. **C.** felony. (CGC 8214.2)

15. **B.** a misdemeanor. (CGC 8221)

16. **C.** shall not charge a fee. (CGC 6108)

17. **C.** not required …. not required (Notary Handbook)

18. **B.** No. (California Civil Code 1185(b))

19. **C.** The credible witness does not personally know the signer. (This is wrong because the credible must swear or affirm that the credible witness **DOES** personally know the signer. (Civil Code section 1185(b)(1)(A)(i)-(v))

20. **C.** perjury (California Civil Code 1189(a)(2))

21. **B.** subscribing (Code of Civil Procedure 1935)

22. **C.** the county clerk (in the county of residence of the notary public). (Family Code 530)

23. **D.** does not remove the personal liability of a notary for claims against the notary. (Notary Handbook)

24. **D.** all the above (Notary Handbook)

25. **D.** No. There is no prescribed wording for the oath. (There are only "acceptable" oaths such as, "Do you swear or affirm that the statements in this document are true?" The raising of the right hand by the notary and oath taker are suggested. However, there is no legal requirement that this must be done.) (Notary Handbook)

26. **B.** the notary may do so because he is only notarizing the signature. Notary Handbook)

27. **D.** $75,000 (Penal Code 115.5)

28. **C.** sending a letter of resignation to the Secretary of State. (Notary Handbook)

29. **D.** A notary public is prohibited from practicing law unless he is a licensed California attorney. (CGC section 8214.1(g)) California Business and Professions Code section 6215)

30. **C**. felony (Penal Code 115.5(b))

"The will to win, the desire to succeed, the urge to reach your full potential... these are the keys that will unlock the door to personal excellence."

-Confucius

PRACTICE EXAM 4

1. The geographical jurisdiction of a notary (the geographical area where a notary can act in his official capacity) is:
A. only the county where the notary oath and bond are filed.
B. only the county where the notary oath and bond are filed and the surrounding counties.
C. only the county of residence of the notary public.
D. all the counties in the State of California.

-----

2. A person applying for a notary commission must complete satisfactorily a course approved by the Secretary of State of California. The course is ___ hours long.
A. 3   C. 9
B. 6   D. 12

-----

3. Which of the following statements is not correct? In a jurat the notary public certifies the following:
A. the identity of the signer based on "satisfactory evidence."
B. the signer signed in the presence of the notary.
C. an affirmation or oath was administered by a witness.
D. the identity of the signer.

-----

4. Which one of the following statements is not correct? A person appointed to be a notary in a military reservation must:
A. be not less than 21 years of age.
B. be a United States citizen
C. perform notarial services on a military reservation located within California.
D. be a federal civil service employee at the military reservation.

-----

5. A notary public appointed for a military reservation must charge:
A. the minimum fees.
B. the maximum fees.

C. no fees.
D. none of the above.

-----

6. A notary public:
A. can notarize all incomplete documents.
B. is prohibited from notarizing incomplete documents.
C. can notarize an incomplete document if it will be completed
   later in his presence.
D. none of the above

-----

7. An agreement between a notary and a private employer may
state that the following may be required to be turned over to the
employer?
A. the notary journal
B. notary fees collected
C. the notary seal
D. the notary public seal and journal

-----

8. What is the title of the subpoena that may be served on a
notary to provide his journal for copying?
A. information subpoena
B. lis pendens
C. subpoena duces tecum
D. none of the above

-----

9. Which of the following ID information is not required to be
recorded in the notary journal?
A. the type of identifying document (Example: passport)
B. the serial or other identifying number of the ID document
C. the date of issue or the date of expiration of the ID document
D. the physical condition of the ID document

-----

10. Which of the following is not correct? The notary public must inform the Secretary of State of the loss, destruction, etc. of the notary journal and must include the following information:
A. the notary public commission number
B. a photocopy of the police report (if applicable)
C. the notary public commencement date
D. the time periods of the journal entries recorded in the journal

-----

11. How much can a notary public charge a member of the public for each photocopy prepared in response to a request by a member of the public?
A. 10 cents
B. 15 cents
C. 30 cents
D. 45 cents

-----

12. If the notary needs a new stamp, he:
A. just asks the vendor for a replacement stamp.
B. must take the 6-hour class.
C. must obtain a certificate of authorization from the Secretary of State.
D. none of the above.

-----

13. Documents that are acknowledged may be recorded by the county clerk. Because of this, the seal must be

_____.
A. 4 inches in diameter (if circular).
B. 3 and ½ by 4 inches (if rectangular).
C. used in conjunction with red ink.
D. legible.

-----

14. If the employee notary (of a public employer) resigns or is terminated, this is considered:
A. the same as a renewal of the commission of the notary.
B. the same as a temporary suspension of the notary public

commission.
C. the same as been found guilty of a misdemeanor.
D. the same as a resignation of the commission of the notary.

15. The maximum fee for administering an oath or affirmation to one person and executing the jurat, including the seal is _____.
A. $2
B. $5
C. $15
D. $10

-----

16. The maximum fee that may be charged to notarize signatures on vote by mail ballot identification envelopes or other voting materials is _____.
A. $2
B. $5
C. $10
D. No fee is permitted to be charged.

-----

17. The required notary public bond (which must be filed with the clerk of county) must be in the amount of:
A. $10,000   C. $20,000
B. $15,000   D. $30,000

-----

18. The notary public applicant must state in his application the name of a business only if he plans to _____ of his notarial services for it.
A. perform fifty percent
B. perform a majority
C. perform all
D. perform a third

-----

19. Grounds for refusal, revocation, or suspension of notary public commission do not include:
A. Adjudicated liable for damages due to fraud,

misrepresentation, etc.
B. Misleading advertising regarding notarial powers.
C. The practice of law, where notary is not a California attorney.
D. Charging less than the statutory fees.

20. Which of the following is not a correct maximum civil penalty for the stated offense committed by a notary?
A. willful failure to discharge notary public responsibilities: $1,500
B. Failure to report to the Secretary of State a lost seal: $1,500
C. Failure to obtain required thumbprint: $1,500
D. Failure to obtain required satisfactory evidence: $10,000

-----

21. If a person is convicted of any crime relating to misconduct on the part of the notary, the court must:
1) revoke the notary commission, and
2) order the notary to surrender the notary seal to the court.
A. 1 only is correct.   C. 1 and 2 are both correct.
B. 2 only is correct.   D. 1 and 2 are both incorrect.

-----

22. The submission of fingerprints by notary public applicants is required:
A. only for the first time a person applies for the notary public commission.
B. every time a person applies for a notary public commission, even if the person held a previous commission.
C. only if the person has been convicted of a misdemeanor or felony.
D. only if the person has been convicted of an infraction, misdemeanor, or felony.

-----

23. A person who intentionally destroys notary public records belonging to a notary is guilty of:
A. an infraction.
B. a misdemeanor.
C. a felony.
D. none of the above

24. A person who influences a notary to do an improper act is guilty of a(n) _____.
A. infraction
B. misdemeanor
C. felony
D. unethical conduct

-----

25. Every officer authorized by law to make or give any certificate or other writing is guilty of _____ if he or she makes and delivers as true any certificate or writing containing statements which he or she knows to be false.
A. an infraction
B. a petty offense
C. a misdemeanor
D. a felony

-----

26. Which of the following two statements are correct? A notary may take an oral deposition by:
   1) writing it longhand, or
   2) typing it on an electronic device.
A. Only 1 is correct.
B. Only 2 is correct.
C. Both 1 and 2 are not correct.
D. Both 1 and 2 are correct.

-----

27. A current passport issued by the U.S. does not have to have the description of the person to be acceptable ID.
A. True, only if the passport was issued in the past 4 years.
B. True, in all cases.
C. False. It is not acceptable.
D. none of the above

-----

28. A notary public who fails to obtain required satisfactory evidence shall be subject to a civil penalty not exceeding _____.

A. $750
B. $1,500
C. $2,500
D. $10,000

-----

29. The "_____ statement" is part of the Certificate of Acknowledgment. It states the county where the acknowledgment is being made.
A. Location
B. Locality
C. Vendor
D. Venue

-----

30. Which of the following statements are false?
If a notary completes an acknowledgment that includes statements which the notary is aware are false, the notary:
A. may be liable for administrative action.
B. may charge more than the statutory fee.
C. may be liable for civil penalties.
D. may be guilty of a criminal offense.

PRACTICE EXAM 4
ANSWERS

1. **D.** all the counties in the State of California. (CGC 8200)

2. **B.** 6 (CGC section 8201(a)(3))

3. **C.** an affirmation or oath was administered by a witness. (This is NOT correct because it should read, "an affirmation or oath was administered by **the notary**.) (CGC 8202)

4. **A.** be not less than 21 years of age. This is not correct. The correct age is 18.) (CGC 8203.1)

5. **C.** no fees. (CGC 8203.6)

6. **B.** is prohibited from notarizing incomplete documents. (CGC 8205)

7. **B.** notary fees collected (CGC 8205(b)(2))

8. **C.** subpoena duces tecum (CGC 8206 (d))

9. **D.** the <u>physical condition</u> of the ID document This is not correct because it is not one of the items listed in CGC 8206(a)(2)(D))

10. **C.** the notary public commencement date (This is not correct. It should read, the notary public <u>expiration</u> date.") (CGC 8206(b))

11. **C.** 30 cents per photocopy page (CGC 8206(c) and 8206.5)

12. **C.** must obtain a certificate of authorization from the Secretary of State. (CGC 8207.3(e))

13. **D.** legible. (CGC 8207)

14. **D.** the same as a resignation of the commission of the notary. (CGC 8200)

15. **C.** $15 (CGC 8211)

16. **D.** No fee is allowed to be charged. (CGC 8211)

17. **B.** $15,000 (CGC 8212) (The notary is personally liable for

all damages. Also, if damages are due to negligence or misconduct, the notary may be required to reimburse the bond company.)

18. **B.** perform a majority (CGC 8201.5 and 8213.5.)

19. **D.** Charging less than the statutory fees. (This should read, "Charging more than the statutory fees.") (CGC 8214.1 (h))

20. **C.** Failure to obtain required thumbprint: $1,500 (The correct maximum civil penalty is $2,500.) (CGC 8214.15)

21. **C.** 1 and 2 are both correct. (CGC 8214.8.)

22. **B.** every time a person applies for a notary public commission, even if the person held a previous commission. (Notary Handbook)

23. **B.** a misdemeanor. (CGC 8221)

24. **B.** misdemeanor. (CGC 8225)

25. **C.** a misdemeanor (CGC 6203) A prosecution for this misdemeanor offense must be commenced (started) within 4 years.

26. **D.** Both 1 and 2 are correct. (Civil Code 14)

27. **B.** True, in all cases. (California Civil Code 1185(b)(3))

28. **D.** $10,000 (Civil Code 1185(b)(B))

29. **D.** Venue (Notary Handbook)

30. **B.** may charge more than the statutory fee. (A notary CANNOT notarize such a document and CANNOT charge a fee. (Civil Code 1189(a)(2))

PRACTICE EXAM 5

1. Generally, a person who wants to be appointed as a California notary must be a California resident at the time of appointment. One exception to this is a person who:
A. is a war veteran.
B. is over the age of 65.
C. is appointed to serve on a military or naval reservation.
D. None of the above are correct.

2. What is the title of the certificate where a person swears (or affirms) that the contents of the document are true and correct?
A. acknowledgment
B. deposition
C. jurat
D. none of the above

-----

3. To be acceptable, a foreign passport must have been stamped by:
A. the California Secretary of State.
B. the FBI.
C. the U.S. Immigration or Naturalization Service or the U.S. Citizenship and Immigration Service.
D. none of the above

-----

4. The term of office of a notary public is:
A. 3 years (if the notary qualified with a 3-hour course).
B. 6 years.
C. 2 years.
D. 4 years.

5.An agreement between a notary and a private employer may state that which of the following may be required to be turned over to the employer?
A. the notary journal
B. notary fees collected
C. the notary seal
D. the notary public seal and journal

6. How many days does a notary have to answer a written request for information from the California Secretary of State?
A. 10 days
B. 15 days
C. 20 days
D. 30 days

-----

7. The notary public journal must be surrendered:
A. to any employer, even if the notary has not worked for that employer.
B. to the county vital statistics office and the county real estate tax office.
C. to a peace officer investigating a crime who has reasonable cause to believe the journal contains evidence of the criminal offense.
D. none of the above.

-----

8. Which of the following two statements are correct? A notary public can complete an acknowledgment:
1. that was mailed to him, but where the person did not appear before the notary.
2. that was mailed to him by a person the notary knows personally, even though the person did not appear before the notary.
A. 1 only is correct.   C. 1 and 2 are both incorrect.
B. 2 only is correct.   D. 1 and 2 are both correct.

-----

9. Which of the following statements regarding a single credible witness is not correct? The single credible witness must sign the notary journal, or the notary must indicate in the journal all the following:
A. the type of ID presented by the credible witness
B. the identification number of the ID document
C. the issuance date or expiration date of the ID document
D. the home address of the credible witness

10. How many days does a notary public have to respond to a written request from a person for a photocopy of a line item in his journal?
A. 10 business days
B. 10 calendar days
C. 15 business days
D. 15 calendar days

-----

11. When a notary surrenders his journal to a peace officer, he must obtain a receipt. The notary is also required to notify the Secretary of State within _____ by certified mail.
A. 5 days
B. 10 days
C. 15 days
D. 20 days

-----

12. Which of the following statements regarding what a notary public seal must contain is not correct?
A. It must contain the name of the county where the oath of office and bond of the notary are filed.
B. It must contain the commencement date of the notary public's commission.
C. It must contain the commission number of the notary.
D. It must contain the ID number assigned to the seal manufacturer or vendor.

-----

13. If the seal of a notary is misplaced, lost, broken, damaged, destroyed or becomes unusable, the notary must give written notice to the _____ who will (within 5 days) issue a certificate of authorization for the notary to acquire a new seal.
A. county clerk
B. State Professions Office
C. county court
D. Secretary of State

-----

14. The notarial fees listed in Government Code 8211 are:
A. minimum fees.
B. suggested fees.
C. maximum fees.
D. average fees.

-----

15. The maximum fee per line item copied from the notary public's journal is _____.
A. 10 cents per copy page
B. 20 cents per copy page
C. 30 cents per copy page
D. none of the above

-----

16. The maximum fee for an acknowledgment or proof of a deed (or other instrument, including the seal and writing the certificate) is _____ for each signature acknowledged.
A. $10
B. $15
C. $20
D. $30

-----

17. A notary who submits an application for a name change to the Secretary of State must within _____ from the date that the amended commission is issued, file a new oath of office and an amendment to the bond with the county clerk in which the principal place of business is located.
A. 10 days   C. 20 days
B. 15 days   D. 30 days

-----

18. Which of the following two statements are correct?
A person who applies for a notary public commission must disclose:
   1. all arrests for which a trial is pending.
   2. all convictions.
A. Only choice 1 is correct.

B. Only choice 2 is correct.
C. Both choices 1 and 2 are correct.
D. Neither choice 1 nor choice 2 is correct.

-----

19. Which of the following is not a correct maximum civil penalty for the stated offense committed by a notary?
A. failing to administer the oath or affirmation: $750.
B. executing a false certificate: $750
C. failing to respond to the Secretary of State within 30 days: $750
D. using the words "notario publico": $1,500

-----

20. The civil penalty for failure to provide access to a sequential journal when properly requested by a peace officer is an amount not exceeding $_____.
A. $500
B. $1,000
C. $1,500
D. $2,500

-----

21. If the last day for the performance of any act provided or required by law to be performed within a specified period of time is a holiday, then that period is hereby extended to and including

_____.
A. the holiday.
B. the next day that is a holiday.
C. the day before the holiday
D. the next day that is not a holiday.

-----

22. A notary who translates "Notary Public" as "notario publico" in the Spanish language is subject to suspension of his notary public commission for one year (for the first offense) and for the second offense:
A. suspension of commission for two more years.
B. fine of $10,000.

C. revocation of commission.
D. none of the above

-----

23. A notary public who is a qualified and bonded immigration consultant may enter data provided by the client on immigration forms and may charge each client $_____ for each set of forms.
A. $15
B. $20
C. $30
D. $40

-----

24. For services rendered relating to an affidavit, or application relating to the securing of a pension (including a Veterans Pension) or the payment of a pension voucher, the notary:
A. may charge $10 for each document.
B. may charge a maximum of $30.
C. shall not charge a fee.
D. none of the above

-----

25. When is a seal not required for acknowledgments?
A. acknowledgment done out of county.
B. acknowledgment done for a non-citizen.
C. acknowledgments on California subdivision maps.
D. None of the above.

-----

26. A proof of acknowledgment of an instrument may be made before a notary public and all the following, except:
A. a clerk of a superior court
B. a county clerk
C. a retired court administrator
D. a retired judge of a municipal or justice court

-----

27. Which of the following choices is not correct? "Satisfactory evidence" means lack of information causing a reasonable person to believe the individual is not the person he claims to be, and:
A. proper ID documents are presented, or
B. the oath of a single credible witness, or
C. the oaths of two credible witnesses, or
D. the presentation of an original social security card.

-----

28. Which of the following choices is correct?
When a notary completes a jurat, he is certifying:
A. the identity of the signer.
B. that the signer acknowledged that he did not sign the document.
C. that the signer appeared in front of the notary in the county specified in the acknowledgment and on the specific date that is indicated.
D. that the signer is over the age of 18.

-----

29. In a certificate of acknowledgment, the notary certifies that he
1) verified the identity of the signer, and that
2) the signer is a resident of that county.
A. 1 only is correct.   C. 1 and 2 are both correct
B. 2 only is correct.   D. 1 and 2 are both incorrect.

-----

30. If a person (a "principal") has signed a document, but does not appear in front of the notary, he can have another person ("_____") appear to prove that the person signed the document.
A. "subscribing witness"   C. a "juror"
B. a "next friend"   D. none of the above

PRACTICE EXAM 5
ANSWERS

1. **C.** is appointed to serve on a military or naval reservation. (CGC 8201(a)(1) and 8203.1)

2. **C.** jurat (CGC 8202)

3. **C.** the U.S. Immigration or Naturalization Service or the U.S. Citizenship and Immigration Service. (California Civil Code 1185(b)(4))

4. **D.** 4 years. (CGC 8204) (Required class and exam must be retaken every four years before the expiration of the term.)

5. **B.** notary fees collected (CGC 8205(b)(2))

6. **D.** 30 days (CGC 8205(b)(2))

7. **C.** to a peace officer investigating a crime who has reasonable cause to believe the journal contains evidence of the criminal offense. (CGC 8206 (d))

8. **C.** Numbers 1 and 2 are both incorrect. (The person MUST personally appear before the notary public.) (CGC 8206)

9. **D.** the home address of the credible witness (Not correct because it is not a requirement of the law (CGC 8206(a)(2)(D)).
The requirements (A, B, and C) also apply when there are two credible witnesses.) (CGC 8206(a)(2)(E)).

10. **C.** 15 business days (Even if no such journal entry exists, the notary public must still respond within 15 business days.) (CGC 8206 (c))

11. **B.** 10 days (CGC 8206(d).)

12. **B.** It must contain the commencement date of the notary public's commission. (This is not correct because the seal must contain the date of **EXPIRATION** of the notary public's

commission.) (CGC 8207)

13. **D.** Secretary of State (CGC 8207.3) (Willful violation may be punished by fine not to exceed $1,500.)

14. **C.** maximum fees. (A notary may if he wishes, charge a smaller fee, or no fee at all.) (CGC 8211)

15. **C.** 30 cents per copy page (CGC 8211)

16. **B.** $15 (CGC 8211)

17. **D.** 30 days (CGC 8213)

18. **C.** Both choices 1 and 2 are correct. (CGC 8214.1(a))

19. **B.** executing a false certificate: $750 (The correct maximum civil penalty is $1,500.) (CGC 8214.15)

20. **D.** $2,500 (CGC 8214.21)

21. **D.** the next day that is not a holiday. (Code of Civil Procedure 12a)

22. **C.** revocation of commission. (CGC 8219.5)

23. **A.** $15 (CGC 8223)

24. **C.** shall not charge any fee. (CGC 6106 and 6107)

25. **C.** acknowledgments on California subdivision maps. (The reason is that the surface of these maps does not work correctly with ink used for seals.) (CGC section 66436 (c))

26. **C.** a retired court administrator (This should read, "A court administrator.") (Civil Code 1181)

27. **D.** the presentation of an original social security card. This choice is not correct because it is not a part of the "satisfactory evidence" definition. (Civil Code 1185(b)(3), (4))

28. **A.** the identity of the signer. (Notary Handbook)

29. **A.** 1 only is correct. (Civil Code 1189)

30. **A.** "subscribing witness" (Code of Civil Procedure 1935)

NOTARY PUBLIC JOURNALS

(LARGE ENTRIES)

1 Service: ☐ Acknowledgment ☐ Oath/Affirmation ☐ Jurat ☐ Other/See Notes Fee $_____ Travel_____			
Name (print)	Document type /Doc. name	Witness Name (print)	Date and Time Notarized _____ ____ ____ am / pm
Phone # / E-mail	Date of document	Witness Phone # / E-mail	Print of Right Thumb
Address	Satisfactory evidence of ID ☐ Driver's license ☐ Known Personally ☐ Credible Witness(es) ☐ Passport ☐ I.D. Card ☐ See Notes	Witness Address	
☐ I.D. Issued by ☐ I.D. Number	☐ Expiration Date ☐ Issue Date	Notes	
Signer Signature		Witness Signature	

Large book (8&1/2 by 11)
2 entries on a page
Total of 250 entries.

NOTARY PUBLIC JOURNAL OF NOTARIAL ACTS

(LARGE ENTRIES AND 2 WITNESSES)

Journal Entry No. 1		
Signer Information	**Witness Information**	**Document & Other Information**
Name (print)	Witness #1 Name (print)	Document type / Document name
Phone # / E-mail	Witness #1 Phone # / E-mail	Date of document ___/___/___
Address	Witness #1 Address	Date & Time Notarized ___/___/___ ___:___ AM / PM Fee $ _____ Travel $ _____
Signature of Signer	Witness #1 Signature	Notary Service Performed: □ Acknowledgment □ Oath/Affirmation □ Jurat □ Other/See Notes
Satisfactory evidence of Identity: □ Driver's license □ Passport □ Known Personally □ I.D. Card □ Credible Witness(es) □ Other (Notes)	Witness #2 Information Witness #2 Name (printed) Witness #2 Phone # / E-mail	Print of Right Thumb (or other digit, if applicable) ▶
Identification document details: □ Issued by: _____ □ I.D. Number _____ □ Expiration Date _____ □ Issue Date _____	Witness # 2 Address Witness # 2 Signature	Notes

Large book (8&1/2 by 11)
2 entries on a page
Total of 300 entries.

CALIFORNIA NOTARY PUBLIC / 235

NOTARY PUBLIC JOURNAL

(600 ENTRIES)

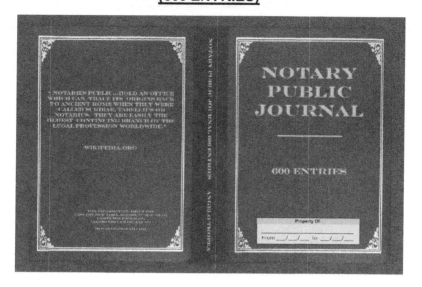

1	Service:	☐Acknowledgment	☐Oath/Affirmation	☐Jurat	☐Other/See Notes	Fee $	Travel $
Name (print)		Document type / Document name		Witness Name (print)		Print of Right Thumb	
Phone # / E-mail		Date of document		Witness Phone # / E-mail			
Address		Satisfactory evidence of ID: ☐ Driver's license ☐ Passport ☐ Known Personally ☐ I.D. Card ☐ Credible Witness(es) ☐ See Notes		Witness Address		Date & Time Notarized _____ am/pm	
Signer Signature		☐ ID Issued by .... ☐ I.D. Number .... ☐ Expiration Date .... ☐ Issue Date		Witness Signature		Notes	

2	Service:	☐Acknowledgment	☐Oath/Affirmation	☐Jurat	☐Other/See Notes	Fee $	Travel $
Name (print)		Document type / Document name		Witness Name (print)		Print of Right Thumb	
Phone # / E-mail		Date of document		Witness Phone # / E-mail			
Address		Satisfactory evidence of ID: ☐ Driver's license ☐ Passport ☐ Known Personally ☐ I.D. Card ☐ Credible Witness(es) ☐ See Notes		Witness Address		Date & Time Notarized _____ am/pm	
Signer Signature		☐ ID Issued by .... ☐ I.D. Number .... ☐ Expiration Date .... ☐ Issue Date		Witness Signature		Notes	

Large book (8&1/2 by 11)
4 entries on a page
Total of 600 entries.

CALIFORNIA NOTARY PUBLIC / 236

NOTARY PUBLIC JOURNAL

(LARGE 2-PAGE ENTRIES)

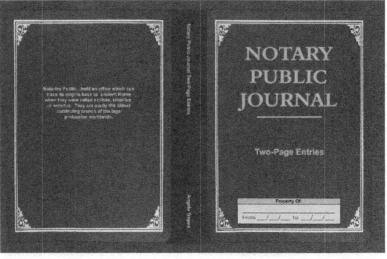

Large book (8&1/2 by 11)
3 entries on a page
Total of 225 entries.

Made in the USA
Las Vegas, NV
22 December 2023